THE ART OF
ASSISTING
AGING PARENTS

Discover the Journey to Honor Your Parents,
Create Treasured Memories, and
Live Life to the Fullest

Teresa Moerer

Paperback ISBN: 978-1-64085-605-9
Hardcover ISBN: 978-1-64085-606-6
Ebook ISBN: 978-1-64085-607-3

Library of Congress Control Number: 2019935015

The information included in this book is for general information and educational purposes only. The content is not intended to be a substitute for professional medical advice, diagnosis, or treatment. It is highly recommended that you consult a physician or other qualified medical practitioner prior to starting any new program for your health including but not limited to diet, exercise, and change in activity level. Likewise, if you have concerns about any medical conditions, treatments, or diagnosis, you should contact a licensed healthcare provider. The information contained herein is provided without any representations or warranties, be they expressed or implied. Mention of specific companies, organizations, or authorities does not imply endorsement by the author or publisher, nor does mention of specific companies, organizations or authorities imply that they endorse this book, its author or publisher. The publisher and the author disclaim any liability for any medical outcomes that may occur as a result of the application of methods suggested in this book.

Some names and identifying details have been changed for confidentiality.

To my Creator—
To you belongs the glory.
Thank you for the gift of life.
Thank you for the daily walk.
I hope I can shine some light on your goodness.

To my parents, John and Rose Mary—
for bringing me into this world,
loving me, believing in me,
and nurturing my gift of faith.

CONTENTS

PART THREE – The Four-Step Method

PART FOUR – The Launch

ILLUSTRATIONS

A NOTE TO THE READER

I believe this book will change your life, and you will change the lives of your parents, family, and friends because you read this book. I don't want to be too presumptive or sound overly confident, but I believe in the fundamentals of the four-step method and the ingredients that go into it—and I believe in you.

The information in this book may seem quite simplistic for some, and to others, it may appear complicated. Trust that the knowledge you need to gain will be present to you at this time. You will continue to increase your understanding of the material as you practice the method. Taking the basic knowledge of the material, applying it, and implementing the method is the key to success.

Committing to read and use *The Art of Assisting Aging Parents* requires you to give of yourself and be transformed as you learn how to provide exceptional experiences for your aging parents.

Although this book is about assisting aging parents, it is also about you. You are not only a stone in the foundation of a family, but you are also a builder. Your success and health are vital to this role and you will find opportunities for growth and development.

After you finish the book, I am confident that you will see life—and caregiving—in a new light, with more hope, more courage, and more adventure.

You are part of the creation. Enjoy your journey!

* * *

Here are a few things to keep in mind as you get started reading the book. The word *experience* is used in part to describe an event you build by combining therapeutic health tools, education, exercise, self-reflection, and other vital elements taught in this book to be used with your aging parents. *Therapeutic encounter, exceptional experience,* and *group therapy* are words that are used in place of the word *experience. Aging parent/s* is the word used to name the person or people you are giving care to.

The word *intelligences* is used early in the book but not fully explained until Chapter 8. It refers to the theory of Multiple Intelligences. If you are not familiar with the theory, know that it describes the many intelligences we possess to gain and use knowledge.

There are many examples of activities and exercises that take place during therapeutic encounters. Some of the activities require a significant amount of strength and balance. Safety is of the utmost importance as you plan and carry out these activities. Start at the baseline of your parents' function with all activities and exercise. Baseline means what they are capable of doing right at this moment. Do not compromise the safety of any participant by attempting an exercise or activity that is too challenging and causes harm to the individual. Ask your parents' doctor for medical clearance for activities and exercise protocols. Their doctor may refer them to a specialist to provide prescriptions and guidelines for activity levels and appropriate exercises. Their doctor may also give them contraindications or warnings against certain activities. Follow their instructions carefully.

ACKNOWLEDGEMENTS

We do not walk this road alone. I want to express my most sincere thanks to the following people and institutions:

My husband, Craig—you know me, accept me, and love me, and I thank you for that. You make my dreams come true. And to my children, Molly, Elizabeth, and Alex—Team Moerer wouldn't be the same without each one of your unique perspectives on life. I am crazy in love with each one of you. You rock my world and always will.

My sisters, Erin, Kathy, Mary, Jenny and their families—you inspire me with your dedication to family and faith. Mom and Dad are proud!

Patty McGrath Crawford—growing up with a best friend was a gift. Thank you for the fun times that still have me doubled over in laughter!

Margo Kreger—an excellent group therapy leader, mentor, and friend.

The beta readers and contributing editors—Ramona Bouzard, Teri Capshaw, Kimberly Groninga, Helen Izek, Nanette O'Neal, Amy Reinhardt, and Abigail Young—thank you for taking the manuscript to the next level.

The creators of Author Academy Elite, Kary Oberbrunner and David Branderhorst; the AAE staff; the AAE tribe; and the Guild—for the support I needed to realize that I could share my message and succeed as a first-time author.

Rockhurst University—for giving me the opportunity to be a part of the first physical therapy graduating class of 1985. And to the leaders who forged the beginning, Ellen, Jean, and Donna— for your inspiration and wisdom.

Sister Rosemary Flanigan—thank you for running in place and stomping your penny loafers on the ground to wake us up and teach us philosophy, and for believing in me.

My co-workers and patients—you taught me about life, love, and persistence. Thank you!

PART ONE:

THE DISCOVERY

1

MY STORY

All artforms are in the service of the greatest of all arts:
the art of living.

—Bertolt Brecht

To take care of aging parents is a source of great joy and an opportunity to participate in another stage of life to its fullest. I know what it's like to make the transition to begin caring for your parents and to continue this care through the end of life. I'm excited to share my knowledge, and I'm honored that you chose to read this book as you start or continue your journey as a caregiver.

I talk to many people who give care to their aging parents. They share stories of memorable times spent together but are quick to point out their frustrations. They convey that much of their dissatisfaction stems from managing busy lives with time devoted to a spouse, family, job, social life, spiritual life, and now the caregiving of aging parents.

Most complaints are fueled by not knowing what care to provide, feeling inadequate in their role, and experiencing burnout. It doesn't take long to sense most caregivers are feeling overwhelmed. The commitment they made to caregiving with anticipation and optimism has turned into a daunting chore. They are seeking guidance and information to improve the lives of their parents while attempting to achieve peace of mind and balance in their own lives.

Finding the right approach to caregiving can be a complicated task and feels paralyzing at times. Recent medical advancements and research provide knowledge, protocols, and treatments to improve health and wellness. We are inundated daily with the latest information on how to change the state of our health. Although this information is valuable, questioning ourselves constantly as to whether we should be adding these new solutions to our lives—as well as the lives of our loved ones—is mentally exhausting. Even if we would like to opt for a change, our fast-paced lifestyles do not allow much time to squeeze one more activity onto our calendars, and our healthcare budgets may be at their limit.

It is easy to fall into the trap of daydreaming about a pill or magic elixir that eases our responsibilities and fixes the aging process. However, when we slow down and become honest with ourselves, we realize we do have to pay attention, work daily on our health, and assist our parents, to the best of our abilities, to reach their highest state of health and well-being.

I have spent some time reflecting on my life and the experiences that paved the way for me to develop and express my passion for helping people reach their highest state of being. One of my earliest memories of wanting to help people dates back to when I was about seven years old and a family in our neighborhood was struggling to make ends meet. It affected me emotionally to watch them and a few other families suffer from poverty, lose children to illness, or end up divorced (which was rare in the 1960s). I remember feeling compassion, empathy, and the desire to go out into the world with a giving spirit. The feelings stayed with me and had an impact on my decision to pursue the profession of physical therapy, which satisfied my interest in medicine and my desire to help others recover from illnesses and injuries. The years I spent in this profession have given me an in-depth and well-rounded understanding of healthcare, healing, and family dynamics.

Another influence I had was the pleasure of working with many talented professionals, including a fantastic group of therapists, who made multidisciplinary group therapy into the most wonderful learning and teaching experience imaginable.

Finally, I have witnessed firsthand the joys and frustrations of caregiving for my parents. The combination of life experiences, my profession, and the caregiving I provide has propelled me to share what I have learned about useful health resources and methods for achieving optimal health.

The process of group therapy caught my attention when I worked in a nursing home that provided skilled care rehabilitation. Patients who were discharged from the hospital after surgery or illness were admitted to rehabilitation where they worked with therapists to achieve their highest level of function before returning home or to another form of housing. In addition to the usual daily routine of therapy, therapeutic exercises and activities were developed for a group therapy treatment session once a week. The groups were multidisciplinary, which meant that physical therapy, occupational therapy, and speech therapy could all be involved in the treatments. The sessions were planned, within insurance guidelines, so all of the therapists were working together but striving for separate goals to suit each patient's needs.

My exposure to group therapy was limited to groups that included patients who had the same diagnosis, the same goals, and the same treatment. For example, the patients who had total knee replacement surgery were placed into a group to do exercises with a physical therapist. The multidisciplinary group was a new concept for me, and I had no idea what to expect.

The first group therapy treatment session I was involved in included exercise as well as a word-building game. The group leader set up an easel that held a large tablet of paper. Therapists were preparing to assist the patients who formed a semicircle around the easel. They were engaging the patients in conversations. I noticed the residents were quiet, and most had a degree of dementia. Stretching and strengthening exercises were started. After the exercises, the lead therapist began to explain the word-building game. I stepped out into the hall to assist a patient in a wheelchair into the therapy gym.

When I returned a few moments later, I looked up at the easel and saw there were approximately 75 words written on the tablet. In the next few minutes, the words increased to 120. The residents not only started speaking but even competing in this game. The page had to be flipped over as they continued to shout out words they made out of a few letters. The facilitating therapists were present but appeared to be mostly inactive. However, they were using simple yet powerful techniques to stimulate the bodies and minds of their patients.

There was an awakening taking place that took me by surprise. It was not only an awakening of the patients but also of this fairly seasoned therapist. It appeared as if nothing extraordinary had happened, but I felt as if I had struck gold. It was my *Aha!* moment. Something was happening that I had not encountered before in therapy. I had witnessed the power of group therapy. My paradigm shift had started—and I was excited to take part in the process again.

I enjoyed the collaborative effort as we developed and implemented comprehensive programs for group therapy sessions. In addition to the physical exercise, the sessions provided opportunities for self-reflection, goal setting, processing, and sharing. I saw terrific events happen as residents became teachers to others and increased their use of social skills. Group therapy provided multiple avenues for learning and communicating. This process sharpened memory for home exercise programs and gave them opportunities to improve their overall functional mobility.

The group would often take on a life of its own, as seen in Picasso's Painting Party in Chapter 13. We would often call this the *magic,* and it was fun to observe the direction the group was taking due to interactions amongst the members. Watching the incredible process unfold each week inspired me to create a four-step method to be able to apply a sequence to the group experience that would further promote the growth of the whole person during rehabilitation and recovery.

The four-step method was developed and then refined using theories, current research, and 34 years of experience in the health care industry as a physical therapist. This book brings together these beneficial therapeutic techniques, education theories, and health tools to promote the development of a healthier body, brain, and spirit. In addition to learning these tools, there is a step-by-step format to use to apply these techniques to your parents' daily routine. Embracing and using this method helps your parents develop healthy habits, set goals, and participate in activities that place them on the path to successful aging. As your parents progress with their health and functional mobility, they can use the method to add programs that interest them or the latest research-based, cutting edge protocols that provide value and meaning to their lives.

My four-step method provides a way to impact your parents positively through the use of experiences. Get ready to learn how to take the resources and use them to create exceptional therapeutic encounters. If you already use some form of this method, you can find ways to improve what you currently provide. By starting this process during the early aging years, your parents have a better chance to age successfully, and you find that your responsibilities as a caregiver decrease. The ultimate result is a higher quality of health for all who are involved.

Using the four-step method bridges the gap between having the resources and knowledge of what to do for successful aging and implementing the process. You and your parents are the builders of the experiences. Through the use of my format plus your knowledge and imagination, you can personalize the activities that work well for you and your parents.

The Art of Assisting Aging Parents aims to teach you the art of building exceptional experiences. I am a physical therapist who has a creative side and loves viewing and participating in art. I'm also a creative artist who is a physical therapist. I spent many years as a physical therapist who was slightly frustrated that my career was not in a more creative field. How did I deal with this dilemma? I made the profession into an art form for myself. With the use of innovation, transformation, and the many therapeutic healing techniques I embrace, I lead people to a higher status of mobility and function.

At times I get so engrossed in my work as an artist of physical therapy that I am in *flow*. When this happens, I know I am part of a transformative process. There is an art to creating your life, home, and surroundings. Not only in the decor but in the daily relational volleying of ideas, humor, and meaningful substance that make us human. Art is complex and is interpreted by an individual on a personal level. It elevates you to your higher self as it draws upon your whole being during your appreciation and interpretation. Art makes experiences more meaningful and should have a place in our lives. I hope you see the significance of this and embrace the art of caregiving.

I have been fortunate to be able to assist family members, to some extent, with the care of my father and mother as they aged. I am full of admiration and pride as I see the actions my sisters and our families have taken to assist our father in his aging years and to make the final years of our mother's life comfortable and fulfilling. A debt of gratitude goes out to my sisters, who have dedicated a considerable portion of their lives to assisting our aging parents. I thank my husband for selflessly giving me time away from him and our home, after the children grew up and moved on, to travel to another state for a few years to be a caregiver as well as a daughter for my mother. I know that this option is not possible or desirable for everyone. I learned much during my time as a caregiver. One of the most valuable lessons was to keep my desire for exceptional experiences high and my expectations low. I was able to avoid disappointments and take delight in the accomplishments of simple, yet glorious times.

What I learned about myself and others through the years brought me to the point where I could share my thoughts by writing this book. It took years of toil and the love of a family, friends, and a profession to get me to this place. My father, now deceased, offered his five daughters more wisdom than we could ever absorb. I live with his inspiration daily. As I work on this book, I long for my mother's talent and expertise in grammar and writing. She wrote for corporate department directors, created newsletters, and penned biographies for fellow club members, with enthusiasm and joy. I'll never forget watching her sit at the kitchen table pounding away on the typewriter keys with focus and intensity. Although she became proficient with computer skills, she still has a love for the typewriter. She continues to ask me who will receive her typewriter when she passes away. That makes me smile—oh, how she loved to write. I am grateful for the unfailing faith and dignity my parents provided as they taught their five daughters to care for others. In an endearing twist of fate, this book is about what I wanted for my parents—and writing a book is what my parents wanted for me.

This is the beginning of anything you want.

—Unknown

2

AN OVERVIEW

Never believe that a few caring people can't change the
world. For indeed, that's all who ever have.

—Margaret Mead

re you ready to take on the adventurous journey of
assisting your aging parents? Do you want to transform everyday encounters with your loved ones into
extraordinary experiences? Will you be open to using your
imagination and intelligence to build exceptional interactions?
If you answered *yes,* keep reading, because this book is for you.

Although the idea of caring for aging parents is not new,
today's environment presents unique challenges. Due to our
modern times, we are finding that our tight-knit, neighborly
communities are fading away. Many of us live a more solitary
existence. In our hurried society, we don't know our neighbors
well. In fact, in many areas of the country, we seldom see the
people living on our street or in our apartment building. The
days of depending on our neighbors for social interactions
and vital support are dwindling.

In the past, our parents relied on activities in community centers, social clubs, church groups, and with nearby family members to keep them active and fulfill their social needs. Many people grew up—and grew old—in the same town. Your parents may have gone to the same doctor, grocery store, and restaurants for years. The diagrams of their home, neighborhood, and city were well mapped out in their brains. Relationships built within the community provided health benefits that were seldom realized.

Unfortunately, that lifestyle of a well-connected community is transforming into a state of isolation. We are now alone amongst a crowd of people in super-sized shopping centers and automated check-out lines. Our aging population thrived in a culture that is slowly being refaced with changing times and scenery from e-commerce shopping, ever-changing health care providers, and fewer face-to-face conversations.

We are finding out it takes a village to help someone live a long life in a productive and meaningful way. Susan Pinker, a developmental psychologist, has written a book entitled *The Village Effect: How Face-to-Face Contact Can Make Us Healthier and Happier,* which describes how an individual's longevity is related to their social life. Pinker suggests that you should be busy building your village if you want to live long into the future. She states, "In order to build what I call the village effect, you need a community of real friends you see in the real world."[1] Making daily connections with familiar friends and those we have weak ties with such as the store clerk, librarian, and neighbors, is good for your body and brain.[2]

Another study found that interactions with our weak ties, or peripheral members of our social networks, contribute to our social and emotional well-being.[3] The weak ties tend to make us more empathetic and many times are responsible for providing us with recommendations for needed resources such as a new doctor, a job, or the best bakery in town.

In contrast, those who are socially isolated and do not partake daily in human interactions are at risk for increased illness and depression.[4] They are lacking the face-to-face contacts that are responsible for releasing neurotransmitters that have the effect of increasing your trust, lowering your stress, and lifting your mood by giving you a feeling of being on a high.[5] Being lonely is worse for your health than obesity or inactivity.[6] It is not a rarity to find a lonely person; instead it is becoming an epidemic as almost half of the American population report they are lonely.[7] The effects of social isolation alone cost this nation billions of dollars each year.[8]

There has been a response to this problem by those who know that people who do not have social interactions are declining in physical and mental health. Solutions to the issue of social isolation are springing up around the world. One proactive program has college students living in nursing homes to provide activities, read literature, and help residents exercise in exchange for housing. Through the app called Join Papa, you can hire "grandchildren on demand." The company sends a college-aged person to help you with a variety of activities such as taking you to the store, providing companionship, or doing housework.

Electronics are also answering the need to fill the void of loneliness. Some of the electronic devices made in the form of stuffed animals or robot figures provide emotional support for seniors. They may not be alive, but they are present and are a means of communication. They may even remind you to take your medicine. There is also technology that connects seniors to their family via an electronic pad that provides communication through phone, FaceTime, and emails. It can display family photos and videos, provide games, and access the internet. Although nothing is superior to face-to-face interactions, these items decrease loneliness by allowing seniors an opportunity to converse and socialize daily.

Another popular trend gaining momentum is called *aging in place*. People are choosing to stay in their home or obtain a home that suits their needs where they can continue to participate in a neighborhood setting and the activities they enjoy. Staying at home may involve modifications to the interior and exterior design to provide adaptations to make the home accessible. As time goes on and your parents need help to stay in their home, a personal attendant can be hired to assist them with activities of daily living.

Technology for your health will be a big part in the future of aging in place. We are now getting a glimpse of how *smart homes* will do more than adjust your thermostat and alert you to security issues. Engineers, architects, information technology experts, and medical professionals are teaming up to develop the technology to provide continuous, non-invasive, and comprehensive healthcare monitoring in the home. The devices that are made to assess body systems such as heart rate, blood pressure, blood sugar, and mental status may be worn in sensors underneath clothing or be placed in your bed or on your bathroom mirror. Wireless monitors for collecting the data are hidden behind walls. The information received is sent to a central location for evaluation by medical professionals. This service decreases visits to the doctor, may avert medical complications, and provides an overall increase in health and wellness for consumers by early detection of medical problems.

In the future, smart homes will be equipped to perform a multitude of tasks that could range from taking inventory of the food you have in your home to calling an ambulance if you fall. There are predictions that as early as the year 2022, there will be an average of 500 smart devices in smart homes.

Telehealth is a medical model that provides services to monitor and treat patients remotely for minor conditions. Some clinics offer virtual appointments with a nurse or doctor via online video conferencing. This feature allows you to have a face-to-face visit from your own home. For seniors, this means being able to live more independent and active lives from their home setting during rehabilitation as well as everyday living.

The response to aging in place is with the village effect in mind. You can continue to be a part of the *village* you have lived in or, if you don't have the support of a personal village nearby, for a yearly fee in some areas you can be a part of a virtual village. What started in Boston's Beacon Hill neighborhood in 2002 has spread to almost 200 villages across the country with 150 more in progress of development. Do you need a ride to your doctor's appointment? How about someone to watch your dog or pick up your mail for a few days? The virtual village, made up mainly of volunteers in your area, can answer that need. They also provide social groups that participate in outings, meals, and educational seminars. The overall effect of the virtual village is to assist seniors with social and financial housing challenges, which allow them to age in place and thrive in their community. The combination of these programs, home adaptations, and technology supports the ability to age in place.

In addition to paying attention to your parents' physical environment and social life, giving their bodies and brains a boost toward optimal health is an excellent choice. A hot topic in the news lately is brain research. Some are calling the brain the last frontier of the body as research focuses on discovering what makes each of us unique individuals. The mysteries of an organ encased in a bony structure are being unveiled with promising news for our future. The research is providing studies that demonstrate evidence of new treatments that slow down and even reverse the brain's aging process.[9] We are looking toward a future when the brain is like the other organs in our body that are evaluated with baseline studies, have ongoing management of disease processes, and undergo progressive treatments. The time has come for us to take the outcomes of this research into our own hands and use it to challenge, develop, and manage our brains as healthy organs as we age.

Researchers are finding evidence to support what constitutes the essential elements your brain needs to thrive. This information is bringing to light the benefits of healthy living. The focus is on *what is good for the body is good for the brain*. In other words, the exercise we do and the beneficial nutrition we place in our bodies to keep our heart and other organs healthy is also what feeds and heals our brains.[10]

We can now choose to be active participants in this process rather than ending up in our older years wondering what we could have done to keep our brains healthy. Many people are pursuing a wide variety of healthy opportunities to eat the right foods, stay active, and be mindful in their daily tasks. It makes sense to follow the recommendations of prominent researchers and physicians from around the world who are giving a prescription on how to nourish, detoxify, and exercise the body and brain for optimal function during our present and future years. These doctors and researchers have witnessed brain scans and tests before and after the adoption of the prescribed treatments. In light of the increase in dementia, Alzheimer's disease, and the steady growth of the aging population, I feel a sense of urgency among health professionals to get this process started. Part Two of this book teaches you the fundamentals for body and brain health.

Now that you know there are solutions to slow down the aging process and build a proactive program to achieve optimal health, are you curious about what you can do for your parents? I hope so! This book teaches you how to assist them as they transition through the aging process. You can provide experiences to keep their minds and bodies functioning at maximum level. You can also offer support to uplift their spirits as they use their strengths to embrace the challenges, joys, and sorrows they encounter. This can be done through the art of caregiving.

Take comfort in knowing that this book is a gentle guide for you to help your parents during their aging process. Although the science behind the aging process is wonderfully complex, the principles, methods, and techniques you are reading about are practical and attainable. After learning the benefits of movement, education, exercise, sensory stimulation, breathing, reflection, and more, you can help your parents integrate these health tools into their daily lives. My goal is to place the therapeutic process in your hands so you can develop the experiences that are right for you and your family. As your parents gain health and function, you will see life-changing events start to happen. The multigenerational effect of caregiving will create much value in your family's life. You may even be surprised at how much you have to learn from the elderly.

It's essential to view therapeutic encounters with aging parents as a process. There are building blocks to this process you will learn throughout this book. Development of the therapeutic encounters may seem a bit overwhelming when you get started, but by the time you have completed a few sessions, you get into flow, and forming an exceptional experience happens quickly. Keep it simple at first, and don't overthink the process. The brain needs new and challenging activities to keep it strong and healthy. Use your imagination to turn this process into a fun adventure!

Whether your parents are at the beginning of their journey, somewhere in the middle, or at the end of the road, you can learn how to help them enjoy their trip. The joy comes out of living well. I am excited to guide you through this journey with your aging parents to obtain health, happiness, memories, and growth.

3

HELP! I HAVE AGING PARENTS!

Family is not an important thing. It's everything.

—Michael J. Fox

B arring an unfortunate event, we will all have aging parents. The first few times you notice your parents displaying signs of aging can be an eye-opening experience. You may be caught off guard and surprised at the changes you are encountering. These incidents are bound to become more frequent, and you will likely start to feel the need to assist them with the activities they find difficult.

There are times and seasons for all things in life, which includes that of assisting aging parents. For some families, the seasons follow a typical pattern or sequence of events. In other cases, they arrive early and unexpectedly. A particular season may last for longer than expected—or end abruptly. Can you ever be completely prepared for the season you are entering? As much as you may try to be ready for all that lies ahead, you need to be flexible as you encounter unknown factors along the way. The earlier you start the process of preparing yourself and your parents for a successful aging process, the more confidence you will all have as you face the challenges ahead. The following pages illustrate three typical scenarios you may find yourself facing.

THE CRISIS

The phone rings. It is unusual for your dad to be calling so early in the morning. You answer the phone and find your father in distress as he explains that he is in the hospital with your mother. Your heart starts racing as you ask, "Is she okay? What happened?" It turns out she was on a morning walk and tripped on the sidewalk. She fell and landed hard on her left side and struck her head on a cement step. The doctor has diagnosed her with a fractured left hip and a mild head injury.

Thoughts race through your head as you ask questions about her medical status and care. You want to be with them to provide support during this challenging time. You start making plans to change your schedule, find friends and relatives to help care for your children, book an airline flight, and start packing. What began with a traumatic incident has affected your parents' lives and your life dramatically. A new dimension added to all of your lives creates dependency and a new dynamic going forward.

THE DECLINE

You notice that you have to repeat yourself several times during a conversation with your parents. Your mother, who regularly attends her grandson's soccer games, wasn't present at the game this week. She surprised you by stating that she forgot about it. During your weekly visit, you observe your father's face isn't shaved as usual, and his hair is a bit unkempt. You offer to take him for a haircut as you straighten his shirt collar. You have picked up on subtle changes in your parents' behaviors. It is evident that a decline has started. It makes you worry that there are changes on the horizon.

THE END IS NEAR

The aging process is taking a toll and—due to a medical condition—you have been told that your mother's end of life is near. It could be weeks or months that you have to spend with your mom. This is usually a time when medical care is necessary to stabilize your loved one's condition. The next step could be comfort or palliative care—or possibly hospice. Quality time for you and your parents is imperative. Medical and spiritual professionals can guide you as you travel through this stage. It is essential to reach out to others for support for both you and your loved ones.

* * *

Can you relate to one of these scenarios? Has your season for caregiving arrived? You most likely picked out this book because you are on a quest to gain knowledge and make a change in the lives of your parents. There could be a desire to understand the complexities of a situation better—mainly how it affects your relationship with each parent. You may also want to consider how changes ahead affect all of your lives. I applaud your willingness to learn as much as possible.

There may be many reasons why you have or are considering taking on the role of caregiver. It could be out of a sense of love or duty. Possibly you are the daughter or son who lives closest to your parents, has the most knowledge, or has fewer commitments. Whatever brings you to this journey of caregiving, it is important to know your *why*—that is, your reason—for taking on this supportive role.

In the movie, *Still Alice,* a brilliant linguistics professor, wife, and mother of three grown children, is diagnosed with early-onset Alzheimer's disease. Alice's caregiving falls into the hands of her youngest daughter, Lydia. Other family members cannot take on this challenge. Alice's husband is in the middle of a career change and can't handle the emotional crisis. Her older daughter has just given birth to her firstborn, and Alice's son is getting on with his life as a medical student. At the end of the movie in a tender scene, before Alice's mind is completely stolen away by Alzheimer's, Lydia recites a segment of a play she has written. The story ends with souls floating upwards, uniting, and being absorbed into the atmosphere to repair the outer layer. Lydia finishes by reciting, "Because nothing is lost forever. In this world, there is a kind of painful progress. A longing for what we've left behind, and dreaming ahead. At least I think that's so." Lydia pauses, then asks her mother if she liked the play. In a delayed response, Alice emotionally nods. Lydia then asks her what the play is about. Alice has difficulty speaking an audible word but finally responds, "Love. Yeah, love." Lydia agrees. "Yeah, it was about love."[1] They share a moment of understanding, sorrow mixed with joy, and love of the past, present, and future.

Love was the *why* that kept Lydia going day by day. You need to discover *your* why and hang onto it. Some days you need a reminder of your purpose.

You may find yourself in denial as you enter this role as a caregiver. Chances are, this isn't the first time you have been in some state of denial about your parents. In the beginning, most of us thought of our parents as perfect. They could tie balloons, blow bubbles, drive cars, and answer every question we asked. Then they became the strangest people we knew. They said something goofy in front of our friends or joked around with the grocery store checkout girl, and we tried to disappear into our own really bad posture. Later, we heard stories of what our parents did in their younger years from relatives and family friends and refused to believe they were ever so wild and adventurous. At some point, we were even in denial about our own conception because, I mean, *I'm sure they never do that!*

Unfortunately, we were probably also in denial about their intelligence and wisdom as we made our way through our challenging teen years and into early adulthood. In time, we see our parents for the human beings they are. We find they give great advice about home repairs, how to cook a turkey, and what to do about an overbearing boss. They reach out to help us change diapers, push strollers, and show an immense amount of love and care to our children. Some are even willing to adopt those we love as their grand-dogs or grand-cats. We never understand the sacrifices our parents made for us until we experience adulthood for ourselves. This makes us proud of the people they are and helps us know what they went through raising and providing for a family.

When the tables start to turn, and our parents now need us, it's tempting to revert to that familiar state of denial. *This can't be happening to them!* The shocking reality is not only what is happening to them, but what is happening to you. Denial is a coping mechanism, but it will not serve you well in this situation. Your parents are going to need you now as you needed them during your growing years. This is your opportunity to embrace a new stage in life and honor your parents through caregiving.

This challenge must be faced head-on. Your parents are inevitably going to suffer declining abilities. Combatting this by providing their brains and bodies with the best food, sleep, water, and exercise is helpful. Although this strengthens them for the road ahead, they continue to age and continue to change. With this change comes loss—loss of functions, friends, and memories. Eventually, as the process continues, you see that they are not the only ones losing something. You are losing something too.

You might be losing your best friend, fishing buddy, shopping and lunch date, confidant, cheerleader, and, most importantly, someone who gave you life and cherishes you. With loss comes grief, and you will experience it in many ways and possibly at the most inconvenient times.

I can encounter grief when I work in the intensive care unit with critically ill patients who have had their life taken away from them in an instant. Although trauma, pain, and torn-up lives surround me, it is my job to bring energy in my step, comfort in my voice, and confidence in my therapy. I am usually able to keep up with the pace and expectations, but there are times when I meet an individual who reminds me of my family. They may be the same age as one of my children. Or, when I meet them and look into their eyes, I'm looking into my mother's eyes. Some patients I find to be caring and compassionate with the same sense of humor as my father. At these times, I can be overwhelmed with emotions. I bite my lip, hold back the tears, and remain strong—or escape into another room, cry a few tears, and then compose myself. The fact is, inside, I feel the tremendous jumbled heartache of love and loss. These emotions tell me I'm alive with deep feelings for others and myself. It is a gift to be fully human.

As I write this book, I think of some of my experiences with grief. I shed my share of tears during my parents' struggles as they faced disease, loneliness, heartache, and fear. These difficult emotions are part of being human, and I'd rather go through life experiencing humanity at the highest level than play it safe. Although this season of life brings about changes and loss, there is so much to gain from fully participating in it.

On the flip side, there is humor. I love to laugh. Knowing the physical act of laughter brings about health benefits, I make sure I laugh every day. Many of the stories I tell in this book could have a humorous slant if you choose to take that approach. There were many scenarios I encountered with my mother in her home and in the independent and assisted living facilities that quickly turned into a comedy sketch with a couple of tweaks to the story. Some days my imagination got quite a workout as we changed the stories and had a good laugh, at no one's expense.

Sharing laughter with so many others is a treasured memory for me. You can approach life with all the seriousness you need, but in the end, I wouldn't trade laughter and fun for anything. It is the food my soul needs to keep going. Make humor part of this adventure! Smile often and feel the health benefits of laughter.

During this journey, some of us are close, and some are far away. I'm not necessarily talking about distance in miles. Some of us have memories of a functional family filled with love and caring actions, while others have memories of a dysfunctional family riddled with pain and trauma. Most of us fall somewhere in the middle with memories of joy and nurturing on both sides of the relationship mixed with defeat and loneliness as we struggled to become adults in an imperfect world. It may be necessary to keep in mind that the past is the past, and we do not have much, or any, control over the future. This present moment is all we have for certain.

I urge you to take the gift of the present moment and apply the health tools you learn in this book to your encounters with your parents. Although these techniques may not appear to be earth-shattering, I have seen them make an impact on peoples' relationships, mental well-being, and physical function. Every little bit of growth makes a difference in your precious lives and is a starting point from which to build.

Don't set this season of life up as a contest. The best aging parent experience doesn't win! You are human and only have so much to give to others while still taking care of yourself and your family. So relax and focus on the process. Know that what works for another person may not work for you. It takes patience and persistence, but not undue stress. Trust that the rewards of healthy living build on each other and you *will* find measures of success.

This season of life may have crept up on you and your family slowly or appeared suddenly. Either way, this is an invitation to connect with your aging parents and enjoy this time in your lives. What you do for them and with them rewards you with memories to treasure forever.

4

SAIL AWAY

The fishermen know that the sea is dangerous and the storm terrible, but they have never found these dangers sufficient reason for remaining ashore.

—Vincent Van Gogh

Clear the thoughts from your mind and picture a blank canvas on an easel. Now imagine yourself painting a boat on the canvas with the skills of Rembrandt or Picasso. Choose whatever type of watercraft you would like—yacht, cruiser, sailboat, fishing boat, or ocean liner. Set your boat upon a lovely expanse of aquamarine water with the hint of a hazy pink sunrise in the background. Now step aboard the boat. Relax and feel the gentle movement of the water preparing to carry you on an adventure. You are ready to sail away.

Are you familiar with boating? Have you ever been sailing or on a cruise ship? Does being onboard a boat sound like a fun adventure? If you were to take a cruise, what comforts, amenities, and entertainment would you want on your ship? What concerns would you have about your time on board the boat? Do you enjoy being on the water or do you prefer dry land?

Thirty-four million people in the United States alone are in the same boat as you, so to speak, as they care for an elderly parent, relative, or friend.[1] It would be nice if we could all go out and buy or build the same reliable boat with a GPS to lead us on well-traveled waters where we would not experience engine failures, stormy seas, or hidden hazards.

The trip we dream of is to step aboard a fully furnished boat, equipped with the luxuries needed for a relaxing vacation, and proceed to sail away to paradise. However, the reality of our caregiving adventure is that, although our sights are set on the same lovely shore, everyone has a slightly different boat in which to travel. Some boats have a sleek, shiny exterior while others are weathered and worn. Engines vary—some are mighty and powerful, and others are weak and fragile. They both arrive at their destination, in their time. Your boat is unique and entirely yours. Embrace it and gather up your crew of family, friends, and other supportive individuals. Own your boat and take pride in it. Step aboard and catch the crosswind. This is your adventure. This is your legacy.

Now that you have your vessel securely in mind, how do you feel about the boating *tour* you are on with your aging parents? Have you lifted your anchor or are you still aground? Does it feel like you are on course or drifting from port to port? Perhaps you feel awash or lost at sea. Whether you perceive yourself as being a little off course or abandoned without an oar, this really isn't new. You've navigated unfamiliar waters before: the first time you sat behind a panel of lights, levers, buttons, and a steering wheel, for example. Or, if you're a parent yourself, the days and weeks following your newborn's arrival. Caring for elderly parents and meeting their needs is new territory for most of us and can be confusing and frustrating along the way.

This book clears up some of that confusion by giving you a map to plan your trip. You and your parents have the compass and the freedom to chart a personalized course. You are the captain. No one knows better what makes your engine run or your sails catch the breeze than you. Getting started on your adventure with a plan in place prevents shipwreck. *Gilligan's Island,* a television show from the 1960s, is a sitcom about a boat caught in a storm that sailed off course. The passengers found themselves stranded on a deserted island for several years. The seven castaways survived intense, yet comedic predicaments in every show. The viewers enjoyed the hilarity of the adventures they found. That was Hollywood. In real life, it's better to chart your course and be prepared.

Navigating the waters is indeed your own experience. You have a past together with your parents. This is a time to be positive and draw upon the strengths you know to be present in your relationship. Recognizing the weaknesses also helps. You may have a different approach to dealing with stress than your parents. Respect for individual preferences is vital. This is not the time to test rough waters. Get rid of baggage by tossing extra weight off your ship; this assists with smooth sailing. As you start to spend more time with your parents in a caregiving role, you may feel fantastic and fulfilled. Alternatively, it could be a painful and empty journey. Make sure you have support for all crew members—including yourself.

Setting the pace is also up to you and your parents. If you feel the need to speed up and move ahead quickly through a stage, that choice is yours. Lowering your sails and making time to warm up in the sun and breathe in the salty air is also an option when you need to slow down and be gently rocked by the waves.

Whatever course you choose, there are days of smooth sailing on crystal clear waters and days when the waves are crashing over your head. Some days you may find yourself bailing away to keep your ship afloat. The storms you weather, on high seas or shallow ponds, will be opportunities for growth and change. Ultimately, with the dedication given to this process, you will observe a positive impact on your and your parents' lives.

It is also critical to balance your life and recognize when you are overly stressed and headed toward burnout. After many days or months of caregiving, you may need to dock your boat and take a break. Know this is perfectly fine and you are seaworthy. You did not fail. Many variables, such as poor health, dementia, dwindling resources, and depression, make caregiving a challenging experience. Finding your level of tolerance helps you maintain your health. If caregiving is causing you to be seasick, you can resign your position as captain. It is entirely acceptable to provide the care for your parents through other family members, friends, and trusted professionals and enjoy your role as a son or daughter as you make time to visit.

In any role aboard the ship, you can use the techniques in the upcoming chapters to improve the lives of your parents and your relationship with them. These techniques can be employed at any point on the aging journey. In the earliest stage, your parents start to decline minimally in function and need some assistance both physically and emotionally. If you haven't already started your therapeutic encounters with them, this is a great time to do so. Research on brain and body function supports early intervention to enhance the aging experience both physically and mentally.[2]

If you enter the crisis stage, your primary concern is managing health care, housing, and daily care. Your parents are likely recovering and working through rehabilitation in order to resume their lives to the best of their abilities. The therapeutic encounters in this book may be modified to continue serving your parents at this time. During the final decline, these experiences can be adjusted again to suit your parents' needs.

This book provides ideas and practical advice to help you gain the confidence to build and implement therapeutic encounters. Use your notebook to start mapping out the best approach for you and your parents to take on this venture. As you work, remember to be flexible and let your ship roll with the tide. I believe every person is driven by a spirit to express their individuality and creativity. Some readers will eagerly take all of the suggestions and examples and implement them while others modify the activities to personalize their experiences. What's important now is that you lift your anchor and get started making an impact in the lives of those you love.

Back to the painting—you may have to add a few brush strokes after reading this chapter. Go ahead and do that; you know what you need to be successful. Now step aboard. You are ready to sail away.

5

THIS WILL BE AN EXPERIENCE

Life can only be understood backwards,
but it must be lived forwards.

—Soren Kierkegaard

What do you remember most vividly: watching ice skating on television or zooming around the crisp ice rink, breathing out cloud puffs, and hearing your skate blades slice the ice? Which affects you more: a photograph of a gorgeous sunrise or sitting on the grass in the middle of its three-dimensional glory? Experiences have a profound effect on our lives.

Why are experiences important? We need experiences to gain knowledge, solidify current understanding, and help us achieve new skills. In addition to learning, experiences can give us pleasure and satisfaction or even cause us to turn up our noses (see below: leftover broccoli). Enjoyment, satisfaction, and even disappointment make life meaningful. We yearn for experiences where we feel love, happiness, greatness beyond ourselves, strength in our relationships, and fulfillment. We seek those opportunities with our families, friends, and groups we belong to. If we are fortunate, we may even find this in the work we do.

To have an experience you need to take in information. Where do you begin? Let me point you back to you: your body. Our bodies, wonderfully equipped with sensing systems, allow us to see lightning in the dark green sky, smell leftover broccoli, taste strawberries, and feel the warm fur of the cat stretched out in the sun patch on the hardwood floor. We can also hear the clink of the closing mailbox and feel the twirl of our office chair as we turn to rise to retrieve that mail.

The brain is the processing center, which interprets information through a complex network of brain cell connections. The brain is responsible for routing and organizing this sensory input and turning it into feelings, emotions, and actions. Ultimately, our lives are formed and enhanced due to the brain's ability to process sensory information. When providing your parents with experiences that stimulate their minds and help them learn, it is essential to tap into the senses. Planned therapeutic experiences are an excellent way to do so.

Jinsop Lee, an Industrial Design Engineer, spoke about the power of sensory design in his 2013 TED talk, *Design for All Five Senses*.[1] He rated experiences based on the degree the senses were stimulated on a scale of one to ten. Lee argued that the experiences which were the most fulfilling also had the highest sensory rating.

Providing meaningful, challenging, sensory-rich experiences is crucial for the health of your aging parents. Incorporating a variety of activities is also beneficial. Repeating the same mastered skills day after day for several years does not build or even maintain brain function. There has to be enough stimulation to spur the growth of new connections to assist the brain in rewiring itself.[2] The brain needs to be challenged with new sensory stimulating learning experiences to enforce and maintain the plasticity properties of the brain, which leads to successful aging.[3]

Neuroplasticity—the ability of the brain to change its structure and function by making new connections and getting rid of connections it no longer needs—is enhanced during mental stimulation and activity.[4] This is discussed further in Chapter 9. We can infer that little or no stimulation of the brain results in an overall decline in the health of the entire body.

An emphasis is placed on the use of group settings in this book because the right social environment, mental and physical challenges, and dynamics of a group can help provide the stimulation your parents' brains and bodies need. It is important for your parents to find opportunities to incorporate relational experiences and functional therapeutic activities with peers and various groups of people during their weekly routines.

Think of how you feel when you get together with your friends to dine or take part in a social event. Do you leave the outing feeling like a weight was lifted off your shoulders? The laughter, ability to expose your deepest feelings, and the opportunity to share stories is therapeutic and decreases stress—which is vital for optimal function of our bodies and brains. We are wired to be social, and that means we need time to express ourselves, connect with others, and feel validated by others. The group setting also gives your parents a chance to gain the role of teacher, confidant, and caregiver to others.

Knowing your parents is vital as you customize planned experiences. Culture plays a part in the interpretation of an experience. The society and culture we are raised in teaches values and influences how we process thoughts. The perception of an experience is subject to many variables—setting, culture, mood, who we are with, time of day, specific memories, or even the experience itself. Being sensitive to your parents' values is essential.

There are a few things to keep in mind as you start planning therapeutic experiences. The first is how pain may play a role in limiting your parents' activities. For example, if your parent has a very arthritic, painful knee, their ability to walk could be limited, leading to a decline in activity and overall health. Pain can be evaluated by a doctor to determine if there are traditional and alternative medicine treatments that would help alleviate symptoms.

Other factors to bear in mind are endurance and strength. Everyone has a baseline tolerance for activity level and amount of muscle strength. You need to meet your parents at their baseline level rather than set your expectations too low or too high. With guidance from a physical therapist, you can receive assistance to determine your parents' level of strength and activity tolerance and find the best way to help them advance to their highest level of physical health. Or, if your parents are healthy, have no restrictions, and can tolerate activity, start at their baseline and help them increase activity and exercise in small increments. Monitor their response to the exercise and advance as tolerated. If the exercises make them very short of breath, and they find they are overly fatigued at the end of the day, they have overextended themselves and need to decrease the resistance and time spent on exercise. They should have enough endurance and strength to carry out their daily activities with safety and clarity.

Another issue is your parents' mental status. We all have challenges to face and when they seem insurmountable, this can lead to depression. Psychological assistance with recommendations for medications and therapy are useful in helping a person through a difficult time. Mental status can also be affected by other factors such as low vitamin levels, dehydration, and infections which need to be treated by a medical professional. A well-designed exercise program may help improve your parents' mental status. Studies show that exercise helps to decrease symptoms of depression and other mental illnesses.[5]

If your parent has not had a recent physical with their doctor, they should have one before starting the therapeutic encounters. A doctor evaluates all of the bodily systems to find problems or diagnoses that could interfere with your parents achieving their best results. Explain to the doctor that you want to assist your parents to gain their optimal health and that you want to know how much—and what kind of physical activity—they can tolerate.

There is ongoing research looking into the factors influencing physical activity in the aging population. One study found that physical activity among Korean older adults was best promoted by focusing on enhancing self-efficacy, social support, and self-regulation skills.[6] That study also concluded that the effectiveness of motivational strategies, such as self-regulation, depends on the importance physical activity plays in older adults' lives.

Elements for success include the following:

- Quality goal setting
- Social support from friends and family
- Self-efficacy
- Planning and scheduling exercise
- Reinforcement
- Time management
- Self-monitoring

You can increase your odds for success by asking yourself these questions:

- How can I ensure my parents receive social support from friends and family to increase their activity levels?
- Is there a way to plan scheduled exercise sessions for my parents individually or with a group?

- Do my parents need extra reinforcement, or are they internally driven to be active?
- Are my parents managing their time well, or do they need help to schedule their day so they can achieve exercise and activity goals?
- Do my parents have goals set to participate daily in activities and exercises?
- Are my parents able to self-monitor as they plan and carry out their exercise programs?
- Do my parents believe they can succeed in an exercise program?

Keep the factors listed above in mind as you plan and implement your therapeutic encounters. Assist your parents to achieve the skills that allow them to participate in the planned exercises and activities.

After reading this chapter, do you wonder how open you and your parents are to this process? You may have preconceived notions from past experiences about diet, exercise, meditation, and many more of the health principles taught in this book. Is this a time for a transition for you as well as your parents? Would you consider giving up some of your past ways of thinking and doing to embrace a fresh start? You may find that you are learning new skills that you can incorporate into your life to make it better. How can you and your parents be more open to the possibilities that change provides? I challenge you to experience this time with your loved ones fully. Participate in the experiences with all of your senses, intelligences, and emotions as you spend time with your parents.

As you plan the therapeutic encounters, don't get so overwhelmed with the complexities of providing exceptional experiences that you lose track of your purpose: to spend some meaningful, quality time with your parents. Uncomplicated, quiet times can become some of your most treasured memories. My mother loves to solve the daily crossword puzzle in the newspaper. When I was able to spend extended time with her, we would sit together on the sofa every evening and between the two of us (highly competitive people) work the puzzle until every last word was filled in. The most poignant times I remember were when she would lean on my shoulder and relax. She needed me. I was her rock, at least for a few minutes. After resting and gathering up some strength, she would reclaim her independence to carry on at the age of ninety with success and grace.

Experiences don't all have to be over-the-top thrilling to be effective. Take time to explore your emotions during quiet times. Your memories will be full of the peace you shared with your aging parents.

6

READY, SET, GO

Tell me and I forget, teach me and I may remember,
involve me and I learn.

—Benjamin Franklin

We're ready to jump into the second part of this book. This is an excellent place to take a look at the ground we've covered, lay out a map for what you'll be learning as you work through the rest of the book, and look at an example of a therapeutic experience in a group setting.

KEY CONCEPTS FROM PART ONE

As you move forward, I want you to keep some of the most critical concepts from Part One in mind:

- Know your *why* as you undertake the task of assisting your aging parents. Write it down and post it in a prominent place so that on a challenging day you have a reminder.

- Realize that there is something beyond the medical care, housekeeping, and meals you provide for your aging parents.
- Understand that in taking on this task to help your parents age successfully, you will be assisting them with activities that stimulate their body, brain, and spirit.
- Maintain or gain a positive relationship with your parents as you share in the process of successful aging.
- Positively impact future generations as you model how to engage with aging family members.
- Recognize the insight, wisdom, and education your aging parents have to offer to others.

WHAT YOU'LL LEARN IN PART TWO

Part Two of this book targets the components for building exceptional experiences. One of the best ways for your parents to learn new skills, improve their health, and focus on a promising future is to provide exceptional experiences for them. You can teach your parents through interactions, conversations, and activities. The components you will learn about include sensory stimulation, multiple intelligences, experiential learning, breathing, movement, goal setting, transitions, and the benefits of healthy nutrition, hydration, meditation, and sleep.

After you feel confident with the fundamental principles, you can utilize advanced techniques or do research to delve deeper into the specific topics you find helpful or necessary for your parents. Alternatively, if you're short on time—and you are finding yourself stressed at the idea of implementing these ideas and suggestions—you can modify the therapeutic experiences to involve less commitment. As you spend time with your parents, make the time worthwhile to them and to you. They benefit from improved health and function, and you all reap the rewards of creating a positive relationship and treasured memories.

Educator, Maxine Green, says, "I'll tell you the secret to good teaching: make possible an experience without predetermining what that experience will be." There is wisdom in her words. It is best to leave the results of the experience up to the people involved in it. We can't know how an experience will turn out because it will be influenced by the unique qualities and personality of each participant—and how they interact with each other. However, we can make sure each experience is designed to benefit those involved in specific ways.

The following group therapy experience is formatted to provide physical exercise, mental stimulation, social interaction, and is meant to be spiritually and emotionally uplifting. This activity also can be used in a one-on-one interaction.

THE GARDENING GROUP

It's a gorgeous, sunny spring day. Perfect for the gardening group that takes place at ten o'clock in the courtyard. The therapists have placed containers for planting flowers and vegetables, including hanging baskets, large pots, and window boxes on the patio and tables. The brightly colored plants, greenery, and potting soil are set on tables to be available for the group members.

Fifteen minutes before starting, the participants are summoned to propel themselves in their wheelchairs, walk with their walkers or canes, or be assisted by staff members to the designated area. The therapists help them get seated at the table, don gloves and aprons, and apply sunscreen to prepare for the group therapy exercise.

The session starts with greeting the group members, talking about the yearly planting activity, and stating the goals of the group therapy session which include increasing strength, balance, coordination, mobility, cognitive skills, speech, and endurance. The participants are then invited to challenge themselves during the planting session by standing up, working together, reaching across the table or to a nearby planter, and taking on higher-level balance activities as tolerated.

The flurry of activity begins as the participants scoop the dirt with their hands or a spade and fill the pots. They push the soil down and prepare it to hold the small, delicate seedlings. Favorite flowers are found by some as they talk about their love of specific colors or shapes of flower petals. The smell of the earthy soil and fragrant flowers brings them back to a time in the past when they worked in gardens to make their yards beautiful and to provide food for their families.

Group members are assisted to stand and reach to hang the flower baskets, sweep the dirt from the sidewalk, and work on sidestepping and balance exercises as they finish covering the roots with soil and water the plants. The warm sunshine, soft breeze, and chirping birds are therapeutic and help the participants relax and start conversations. They chatter about years spent working in agricultural occupations, pursuing their outdoor hobbies, teaching moments for their children, the flavor and nutrition of home-grown vegetables, and beautiful yards they maintained. The group session winds down and heads into a processing stage where the participants talk about their experience.

The questions could include the following:

- What do you enjoy about planting flowers?
- Do any of you dislike gardening?
- How did you feel today as you planted the flowers?
- What muscles did you use to complete the activity?
- What was your personal goal today during the group exercise?
- What did you do to accomplish that goal?
- Do you feel calm or stressed after the gardening activity?

- How can you relate the experience you had today to an activity you do at home?

The questions lead to conversation, self-assessment, and reflection. The therapists assist group members who have difficulty communicating. All of the comments are acknowledged and expanded on as time allows. The opinion of each person is discussed and validated. The participants enjoy reminiscing during social interaction. They are receiving the tremendous health benefits of decreasing stress and elevating mood.

During this group therapy session, the therapists are working on skills that relate to the goals of each participant. Some of the areas they focus on include the following:

- Balance and coordination
- Muscle strength
- Safety skills
- Insight into themselves, others, and the activity
- Quality of mobility
- Endurance
- Cognitive abilities in following directions and solving problems
- Transitioning the activity to other areas of function
- Participation
- Social skills

The gardening group is an example of a multidisciplinary, multifaceted therapeutic experience. If your parents were participating in the gardening group, what would you be expecting them to accomplish? Keep this example in mind as you read the rest of the book. It is a good reference point when we talk about the senses, experiential learning, the intelligences, and the other tools and methods used to create a great experience.

Setting Goals and Getting to Work in Part Three

Finding regular activities that bring a twinkle of joy to your parents' eyes feels fantastic. To do that, you'll need a plan tailored to meet their particular needs. Maxine Green, quoted at the beginning of this chapter, says, "Part of teaching is helping people create themselves." To remain vibrant, your parents need a plan for life that reflects their unique personalities and makes allowances for their current physical and cognitive status. The third section of this book provides a framework to help design that plan. You can read a brief overview below of the four-step method, so you know where you're heading—and what you're learning—as you continue to work your way through this book.

The Four-Step Method

Step 1: Who I Am
Your parents reflect on their cultural background, past experiences, and strengths during Step 1. As you go through this process with your parents, help them focus on their accomplishments, attributes, and talents. If this first stage is a positive experience, they move forward with a sense of hope and empowerment. This helps them take an active role in their experiences.

Step 2: Life Vision and Goal Setting
This step encompasses your parents' vision for the future. You and your parents focus on what they value and want to achieve during the rest of their lives. After they reflect on the questions provided, they can articulate what they want their purpose-filled life to look like. Begin setting goals that align with your parents' vision or physical needs at this time.

Step 3: Empowerment Through Concrete Activities
Now you can get to work doing what's necessary to achieve the goals set in the previous stage. By reflecting on the questions provided, you can develop activities that relate to the goals. This may include exercise, socialization, meditation, brain training activities, and finding ways to eliminate barriers to their goals.

Step 4: Assessing Therapeutic Activities and Goals
During this final step, you and your parents assess if they are making progress using the therapeutic encounters and are on their way to achieving their goals. The goals may need to be adjusted or changed, depending on your parents' desires and needs. At this time, it is evident if you need outside assistance from professionals such as doctors or therapists.

PART FOUR—THE LAUNCH

It's time to take what you've learned, embrace your *why*, and celebrate the present. This section presents you with the wings—and the sails—to start your adventure and begin this season of life with your aging loved ones.

* * *

As you work through the next three parts of this book, you are a student as well as a teacher. Keep an open mind as you learn the material and think of how to apply it to create exceptional experiences.

PART TWO:

TOOLS FOR EFFECTIVE EXPERIENCES

7

I CAN HEAR YOU NOW!

The five senses are the ministers of the soul.

—Leonardo da Vinci

Snowflakes are swirling around on a cold January day. This blustery weather has me craving one of my favorite comfort foods: Italian spaghetti and meatballs. Our favorite recipe, given to my mother by a good friend, has become a family tradition that is now handed down to the next generation. I go in search of the handwritten recipe in my overstuffed recipe box. As I pick out the well-worn, sauce-splattered index card, I hear my mother telling me how it's essential to use the right amount of sugar to bring out the tomato flavor.

As I proceed to mince onions, press garlic, and scrape the pungent tomato paste out of the cans, the aromas invade my nostrils and promise me a flavorful meal at the end of the day. The muscles in my arms and hands are used to mix and shape the meatball ingredients and stir the deep red tomato paste into the sautéed vegetables and water until it loses its posture and melds into a thin liquid. Opening the oven door sends a blast of heat to greet me as I place the meatballs inside to bake.

Strolling into the family room, I go to the stereo to turn up the volume of a song from the 1970s. The song takes me back to a time filled with memories of growing into adulthood. Throwing a few dance moves into my walk back to the kitchen, I glance over at a picture of my family and feel my heart swell with the immense love I have for them. There are no words for those feelings forged deep in my soul. Approaching the stove, I see the steam rise off of the simmering sauce. The garlic scent wafts my way, and the meaning of comfort food is cradling me. I deeply breathe in and out—and smile at the joys in life.

Ah, the senses. Imagine life without them. It would be rather dull. The above example of sensory stimulation and mindfulness uses every sense to compose a gratifying experience. Can you think of a sensory experience that caught your attention and prepared you for an outstanding moment?

One experience that caught my attention a few years ago was when I bought an Apple Macintosh MacBook Pro. The sales assistant brought my MacBook over in a sleek, minimalistic white box and placed it on the table in front of me. I stared at it as I studied the shape and texture. He smiled and said, "You need to open the box. This is part of the experience Steve Jobs wants you to have."

I was impressed that someone cared to start this process with the consumer in mind. As I lifted the lid off of the box, I noted the tension between the top and the bottom of the box as it was providing gentle resistance to my muscles and joints. As I continued to open it, it felt as if the box was taking in a breath of air. These sensations sent signals to my brain and created the feeling of anticipation of an awesome experience. I was not disappointed. The inside of the box was just as amazing![1]

I still have that box. I don't go by the box very often, but when I do, I lift the lid off of the box. You may think I have quite an imagination, and I do, but the truth is, I'm a sensory junkie!

A few sensory experiences that have alerted me lately were the artistic presentation of a delicious dessert, meaningful music during a worship service, and the look, smell, and feel of a new car. Increase your awareness during experiences and note which senses are stimulated and to what degree they affect you. More information on mindfulness, or how to assist your parents to bring awareness to experiences, is in Chapter 11.

In her book, *Smart Moves: Why Learning Is Not All In Your Head*, Carla Hannaford tells us how we use our senses to learn and form our concepts about the world.[2] She explains that sensory development starts in utero about one month after conception. We first learn about gravity while floating in the amniotic fluid. Our other senses build upon this, and we begin to use them to experience and understand our world. When rich sensory environments surround us, and we have access to explore them, we can build neural networks that enable us to navigate our world and succeed in it. In other words, our brain forms complex pathways in the nervous system if our environment is full of interesting sights, sounds, smells, tastes, movements, and touch that we are able to interact with. What happens next is exciting. From those pathways, we derive images that are played out in our thoughts, learning, imagination, and creativity. The images of ourselves and the world become more complex as we feed our sensory system, add emotions, and movement. New learning occurs as this process unfolds during all of the experiences of our lives.[3]

Learning can be delightful, helpful, and sometimes, even life-saving. Your parents will most likely encounter a time when they need to change how they do something—or get help doing it. One example is walking. A cane or walker may be a necessary assistive device for your parent to use to continue ambulating. When that time comes, they will need to learn how to function in a new way. The senses are a part of the learning experience as they are taught to use the assistive device correctly.

The term, sensory stimulation, is used to describe the activity that takes place to stimulate the senses. There is evidence that using a sensory stimulation program on brain-injured patients has a significant effect on their recovery.[4] Sensory stimulation used with dementia patients also provides an awakening effect. It provides the benefits of increased socialization, concentration, alertness, and improved self-concept.[5] As the stimulation increases alertness and awareness, it becomes a component in building new neural connections. As you plan therapeutic encounters for your parents, keep in mind that stimulating the senses has the effect of alerting the brain, improving the experience, and aids in the learning process.

The six senses we possess are taste, touch, hearing, sight, smell, and proprioception—our sense of self-movement and body position. We depend on these senses to give us the information we need to navigate through each day. If the body has dysfunction in a sensing system, the message is not able to be relayed to the brain. One example is peripheral nerve damage, which means the nerve damage is outside of the brain and spinal cord. Due to traumatic injury, chronic diseases, metabolic problems, and inherited disorders, peripheral nerves can lose their ability to be stimulated so they cannot send a signal.

There are times when the brain cannot accept the signal due to an injury, which may have been caused by a stroke, brain injury, or tumor. This is considered central nervous system damage. If nerve impulses from the sensing organs cannot reach the correct area of the brain, there is no processing of the information, and therefore, no response to the stimulus. At times you may need to make the sensory stimulus stronger or give sensory input through a sense that is functioning so that your parents can make adjustments and continue to function at their highest level.

As we age, our sensory systems lose their acuity and slow down at individual rates.[6] Eyeglasses and hearing aids assist by providing input to your eyes and ears. Your parents may also lose the sense of touch or feeling in their feet, which is an example of peripheral neuropathy. Not having the sensory input or feedback from their feet on the ground affects the ability to balance and increases their risk of falls. They could also sustain an injury to their foot and be unaware of the damage. Your parents have to learn how to compensate for this loss by changing the way they do activities, taking extra safety precautions, and sharpening other senses and systems.

Stimulating the sensory system has positive and powerful effects on the brain if done correctly. As we age, our sensory systems decline, and it is harder to notice details. A certain amount of information from the sensing organs is required before you become aware of a sensation. The minimum amount is called the threshold. Aging raises this threshold, and you may need to provide more sensory stimulation to perceive or be aware of the sensation.[7] For example, your parents may need you to talk louder, turn down the temperature on the water heater to avoid a burn, or spice up their food so it's tasty.

The changes caused by diminishing senses can have an emotional impact. How would you feel if you were to miss out on vital information you needed to be able to function during everyday life? What would you do to make your needs known if your usual means of communication were not sufficient? Would you become impatient and yell out to others for help? Or, would you start regressing into yourself and give up on trying? How would your self-esteem be affected by these changes? Think about how you can help your parents adjust and make accommodations to the sensory changes they experience. Also, keep in mind how important it is to stimulate the senses to keep the neural networks strong so the changes happen at the slowest rate possible.

I have never lost one of my senses, but I did experience losing my voice while attending a three-day conference. The seminar was a combination of lectures and interactive labs.

In small groups, we practiced the therapeutic techniques we had learned. As the weekend progressed and my voice started fading, I had less of a say in the workings of our small groups. This made me feel useless, and I began to withdraw from group interactions. I could not be heard.

There are many ways to communicate. I could have written my input on paper and presented it, but these sessions were fast-moving and did not allow time for that. Fading into the background and feeling useless was frustrating. As I wandered around during the session breaks, browsing the materials available for purchase, I ran into familiar colleagues. It was very disheartening not being able to interact verbally. I remember that feeling of isolation every time I work with someone who has lost a vital function.

Fortunately for me, this was a temporary situation. My voice came back. I did not have to make any long-term adjustments. Your parents may experience the permanent loss of a sense, such as hearing or sight, and they will have to make changes so they can function in new ways.

The six senses are described below, followed by suggestions for stimulation of that sense.

TOUCH

The sense of touch is perceived through the largest organ of our body, our skin. Touch receptors located on the skin relay messages to the brain, which translate as light and heavy pressure, temperature, vibration, and pain. Touch is a powerful sense and can elicit an emotional response that is unparalleled.

Touch is also a way that humans communicate feelings to each other such as compassion. Emotional hugs, a soft touch on your hand, and a pat on the back are affirming and make us feel secure. Deep or heavy pressure into your system has a calming effect, and wrapping a person up in a blanket can give them feelings of security and peace. Touch has also been found to be able to influence our decision making.

Sensory stimulation for touch could include the following:

- Hand massage and manicure
- Pet therapy—petting a puppy or holding a kitten
- Identifying an object placed in a bag by touch only
- Using clay or putty to build a model—also strengthens hands
- Getting your hair done—brush hair
- Sensory bean bags made of various textures and materials
- Hold hands
- Cooking—kneading bread

SIGHT

Our sense of sight is considered our dominant sense. It provides a view of the world and helps us make memories. We use our eyes in combination with our other senses to see. Our brain maps out a picture of an object based on many factors. A very small percentage of vision is processed through our eyes. The rest comes from our senses of touch, hearing, and proprioception. For example, when you want to see something, you often pick it up, feel it, and listen to it. This gives your brain the information it needs to make a visual map of the object.

Those who can't see usually increase the acuity of their other senses to compensate for this loss. With aging, the sharpness of vision declines, and it is difficult to tolerate glare. Make sure your parents have an eye exam and have the care they need to optimize their vision.

Sensory stimulation for sight could include the following:

- Bird watching
- Viewing new scenery outdoors
- A bouquet of flowers in their favorite color
- Videos and movies
- Bright, stimulating colors
- Three-dimensional scenery
- Viewing art
- Painting, coloring or drawing
- Jigsaw puzzles
- Multi-sensory experiences using hearing, touch, and proprioception to enhance the visual experience

HEARING

Hearing is another sense that adds significant value to our lives. At the end of winter, you hear the chirp of a robin signaling the future event of spring, and your heart sings. The sound of the alarm clock can signal the promise of a new day or the dread of getting out of a warm bed.

Playing an instrument and listening to music have been found to have a neurochemical component that increases your immunity, helps you manage your mood, decreases your stress, and aids in social bonding.[8] Music is cathartic and can help you get in touch with your emotions as you heal.

Hearing loss has been found to speed up cognitive decline.[9] It is also associated with increased falls due to the demands that hearing loss places on the cognitive system. An overburdened brain may not have the additional resources needed to attend to the high levels of cognitive requirements needed for gait and balance.[10] Another reason is that you may not be as aware of your environment and surroundings if you have difficulty hearing, which could lead to running into an object, missing a step, or tripping over a rug.

Have your parents' hearing tested and purchase hearing aids if needed. In addition to the issues above, without the sense of hearing, your parents can quickly become isolated, leading to further decline and illness. Shouting at someone for any length of time is frustrating for both parties. When talking to a person who is hard of hearing, you may need to speak into the ear that has better hearing to decrease their frustration. Use face-to-face conversations so your parents can lip read and see your facial expressions. Another way to communicate is by writing down your questions and comments if eyesight is not a problem. A small whiteboard is helpful for this.

Keep in mind that challenging the brain by listening to sounds in a standard volume will affect neural pathways positively.

Sensory stimulation for hearing could include the following:

- Play soothing music or a relaxation CD of the ocean for a calming effect
- Spend time in nature listening to birds, insects, and animals
- Attend a concert
- Take part in playing a musical instrument such as drums, recorders, keyboards and bells
- Mix up varieties of music to include change for optimal brain stimulation, such as jazz music
- Make frequent phone calls to hear the voices of your cherished family and friends

TASTE

I think we would all agree that taste is a sense that brings us much pleasure. My family takes delight in finding, cooking, and sharing exquisite culinary experiences. In other words, we are foodies! We enjoy traveling to small towns to find some of the best burger joints or hitting the streets of a major metropolis to find neighborhoods where you can enjoy the authentic, delicious ethnic food that settles our souls' craving for complex flavors. Ah, what an excellent way to satisfy the sense of taste and stimulate our brains with conversation built around food, flavors, and textures.

Sensory stimulation for taste could include the following:

- Eat spicy, sour, and salty foods
- Taste fresh herbs and vegetables out of a garden
- Prepare foods from childhood recipes
- Enjoy favorite sweets and pastries
- Take a cooking class

SMELL

The sense of smell is a part of taste. It allows us to savor beautiful moments around a meal together, bringing us social interaction and enjoyment of life. We also rely on our sense of smell to alert us to the danger of spoiled food, gases, and smoke. This sense is one of the most meaningful in terms of connecting us to our past and bringing back memories. These memories, in turn, are responsible for our emotions tied to the smells.

I worked part-time when my children were young. During their elementary school years, I wanted them to remember the days when they would come home from school and I was there to greet them. So, every Thursday, I had a batch of cookies ready to pull out of the oven as they arrived home. I knew that the aroma of the cookies paired with sitting down at the table together, talking about their day while eating warm cookies and drinking a glass of cold milk, would be a memory for them. They are young adults now, and I haven't asked them if they remember the cookie dates we shared every Thursday afternoon, but I hope that each time they smell a batch of freshly baked cookies, they feel the emotions of love and security.

Here are some ways to stimulate the sense of smell:

- Use aromatherapy by diffusing essential oils
- Bake cookies or fresh bread
- Display a fresh bouquet of aromatic flowers
- Smell spices during a cooking session
- Open the windows in springtime to smell the fresh air after a rain shower

PROPRIOCEPTION

Proprioception is responsible for letting us know the position and movement of our limbs, a sense of muscle force and effort, and a sense of balance. Receptors for this sense reside in our muscles, joints, and skin. Our brains are continually mapping out where our bodies are in space from the information it receives from this sense. This allows us to move around during the day, completing our tasks without thinking about how to adjust our bodies. If we did not have this sense, we would be floundering around unable to make any purposeful movements without looking at our bodies.

With aging, this sense diminishes, and we may note a decrease in coordination and balance, which increases the risk of falls. Proprioception enables us to control the movements we make and also provides us with our sense of self through awareness of our body and its actions as we navigate our surroundings.

Sensory stimulation for the proprioceptive systems could include the following:

- Walk on uneven ground
- Climb stairs
- Practice Yoga and Tai Chi
- Participate in an exercise class

- Dance
- Carry weighted objects
- Turn your body or head

Sensory stimulation provided daily is what some practitioners call a sensory diet. As we provide our bodies with sensory stimulation, we are *feeding* the senses. Our senses need to be stimulated regularly to keep neural networks strong.

Never underestimate the workings of the sensory systems. I was pushing a patient from her room to the therapy gym in her wheelchair, which I did three times a week. As we strolled down the hallway, I addressed her several times as I had earlier in the week attempting to make conversation. I got the same response as all of my prior attempts—which was receiving no response from her. I assumed that she was either very hard of hearing or that she had dementia keeping her from understanding my words. It was the middle of summer and we were experiencing a typically hot, dry season. As we reached the elevator door, I stopped, looked out the window at the brown grass, and stated, "We sure need some rain." She shot back at me in a loud, authoritative voice, "God *knows* what we need." My eyelids raised, as my head flew back. I was startled by her response. The impact of the periods of silence, followed by a very profound statement caught my attention. I thought about her comment for a few seconds and then agreed with her, "Yes, God *does* know what we need."

Wow, I learned a few lessons that day. One was about the faith of a woman who was patiently enduring her arthritic joint deformities and pain, had most likely seen her share of trying times and had just proclaimed an unwavering faith in God. The other lesson I learned was never to take for granted that the sensory systems of a person are diminished, ever. I can still see her face, hear her voice, and feel the shock I felt 29 years ago. The one comment she made had a profound effect on me and now and then whispers in my ear. I still marvel at her conviction in her faith.

Our senses open the door to a rich and meaningful life. We feel, learn, and grow through our experiences. Incorporating the senses during learning helps build new neural networks and makes learning more memorable.

As verbal skills decrease during aging, especially with the diagnosis of dementia and Alzheimer's disease, remember that connecting with your parents through the senses is a valuable way to communicate. Start thinking about how you can provide input to the senses as you build experiences for your parents.

8

STOP, LOOK, AND LISTEN

Intelligence is the ability to adapt to change.

—Stephen Hawking

Research by Howard Gardner, an American developmental psychologist, on the theory of Multiple Intelligences came to my attention in 1999. As I investigated the theory, I became intrigued and excited. My job as a physical therapist involves a significant amount of communication and education. This theory brings to light that individuals have several intelligences they use to take in information as they learn as well as to express themselves. This appeared to be knowledge I could use in my profession as well as in everyday life.

According to the theory of Multiple Intelligences, we all experience and understand the world in various ways. This "profile" of intelligences includes nine different ways of making sense of what's happening around us. Gardener wrote, "We are all able to know the world through language, logical-mathematical analysis, spatial representation, musical thinking and use of the body to solve problems or make things, an understanding of other individuals, and an understanding of ourselves."[1] However, Gardner argues that while we all possess each of these nine intelligences, the strength of each intelligence is not equal. According to this theory, measuring intelligence based on I.Q. testing is far too narrow. He was concerned that the educational system and our culture are heavily biased toward the linguistic and logical-quantitative modes of instruction and assessment.[2] He believed students learn in individually distinctive ways and they could be taught more effectively if the learning was addressed through a variety of means. By offering an array of approaches to learning, the end result is successful education.

My quest for information and application of the theory continued. I began to understand that the nine ways individuals know and process information are independent but can be interconnected. I use my strong intelligences as I teach and communicate with others and it is evident that my patients have intelligence strengths they are using to understand the instructions I give them during their treatment sessions. At times we are matched up well with similar strong intelligences. For instance, I have patients who share my strengths of intrapersonal and visual-spatial intelligences. When we work together, it is as if we are speaking the same language or seeing eye to eye as the communication and treatment flow well. At other times, it is difficult to find common ground with our intelligences, and there is the potential for both parties to experience misunderstanding and confusion. When that is the case, I appreciate the differences between us and respect their unique strengths and weaknesses as we work together to accomplish the goals.

As individuals know how they learn is valued and accepted, their interest and effort increase during the learning process. We do not always have to match up with intelligences to have a successful outcome. Sometimes it is helpful to have a variety of strong intelligences among a group of people as it balances the work and family environment.

During my therapy treatments, I assess the intelligences of my patients. I do this by asking questions about occupations, hobbies, and interests. I also determine my patients' reaction to various types of learning such as home exercise programs that contain written words and pictures, body awareness, exercises that involve coordination of the extremities, and verbal feedback on the progress of therapy. All of the information assists me to develop a communication and instruction plan geared toward each patient's intelligences. The focus of the treatment plan uses their strengths and also addresses their weaknesses to formulate goals that will help them attain their highest level of function. I am also able to understand how the patient's behaviors relate to the strengths and weaknesses of their intelligences. Many times problems are averted by knowing how they might react to particular circumstances. This approach helps me communicate and educate and it improves the quality of care my patients receive.

As an example, when working with athletes, it is relatively easy to communicate correct exercise techniques because they have high kinesthetic or body awareness when moving. If that same individual has weak intrapersonal intelligence, they may not understand why the exercise benefits them, which could lead to poor follow-through with completing the exercises. On the other hand, a person lacking kinesthetic awareness may have a difficult time learning more complex exercises as they often do not know where their body is in space and they are not accustomed to *listening* to the feedback their body is giving them. If that same person has linguistic, visual, or logical intelligence strengths, I provide handouts of drawings demonstrating the exercise as well as written instructions including details on the exercise techniques. The end goal for the second patient is to achieve improved kinesthetic awareness and, by providing access to learning opportunities that address a variety of intelligences, there is a higher chance for success. The first patient mentioned above is a pro at exercising but needs more education to focus on how the exercises benefit him in his daily life.

The more knowledge you have of your parents' intelligences, the easier time you have communicating and developing beneficial experiences. Remember that to provide a well-rounded learning experience, giving attention to several intelligences is essential. All of the intelligences can be developed and many are needed to master a new skill. The awareness of developing multiple intelligences and the attention to learning fosters growth in many areas of your parents' lives.

Most of us have a good idea of the strength and weakness of our intelligences. After you read the description of the nine intelligences that Howard Gardner proposes, you can go online and find a multiple intelligence inventory to determine your strengths and weaknesses.[3]

LINGUISTIC

Linguistic intelligence is the ability to use and understand language. People with strength in this area tend to like making up stories and poetry, playing word games, reading, listening, and speaking. They have highly developed auditory skills and can think in words. They are often interested in computers, games, lectures, books, and multimedia. Career choices might include writer, speaker, lawyer, or translator.

LOGICAL-MATHEMATICAL

Logical-mathematical intelligence includes the ability to reason and calculate. People with strengths in this area think abstractly. They are also able to conceptualize relationships and understand complex problems using symbols, processes, and actions. To deal with details, they need to learn and form concepts. They like to explore patterns and relationships by using experiments, working puzzles, and asking cosmic questions. Scientists, mathematicians, accountants, and computer programmers are career choices for this intelligence.

VISUAL-SPATIAL

Visual-spatial intelligence involves understanding physical space. Learners with a strength in this area think in terms of physical space and can see and modify things in their mind. They understand the visual world and its relation to physical items. They like to do jigsaw puzzles, draw, read maps, and daydream. Teaching tools for them would consist of maps, photographs, charts, graphs, multimedia, and 3-D modeling. They might choose professions such as architect, sailor, or artist.

MUSICAL

Musical intelligence is an awareness of rhythm and sound as found in music critics, performers, and composers. Those with a strength in this area are acutely aware of rhythm and sound that surrounds them in their environment. They can feel the emotions in music and often have music in the background as they study or work. Expression of this intelligence is seen through singing or playing a musical instrument. Teaching them works well if lessons revolve around speaking rhythmically, turning lessons into lyrics, or tapping out time.

KINESTHETIC-BODY

Kinesthetic-body intelligence is a sense of body awareness. People with a strength in this area have a keen sense of body awareness, as seen in dancers, athletes, and surgeons. They communicate well through body language and movement, making things, and becoming physically involved. This skill is defined as *thinking in action* and is used for self-expression as in theatre or precision to achieve a goal such as a watchmaker or a surgeon. Tools for learning include real objects and equipment used during physical activity, acting out, role-playing, and hands-on learning.

INTRAPERSONAL

Intrapersonal intelligence focuses on inner feelings. Learners with a strength in this area have a good understanding of their interests and goals, strengths and limitations, and awareness of inner emotional moods, motivations, and desires. They tend to shy away from others. They possess a strong will, confidence, and opinions. They are the most independent learners. An excellent approach to working with them might include independent study and introspection using tools such as books, creative materials, diaries, privacy, and time. They value learning, personal satisfaction, knowing oneself, and being on the road to achievement. Career choices could include authors, professors, and philosophers.

INTERPERSONAL

Interpersonal intelligence deals with understanding and interacting with others. People with strength in this area enjoy social interaction and understanding the people around them. They display empathy, street smarts, and sensitivity to the perspectives, intentions, and moods of others. They often use this intelligence to influence a group of people to follow a line of action. They can learn through group activities, dialogues, and seminars. Learning tools include telephone, audio-conferencing, time and attention from an instructor, writing, E-mail, and video conferencing. Career choices may include upper-level management, public relations, and sales.

Naturalistic

Naturalistic intelligence deals with understanding patterns of living things and how to apply scientific reasoning to the world. People with a strength in this area can distinguish between varieties of plants, animals, and weather formations found in the natural world. They usually have very little interest in subjects that are not related to the natural world. They seek out opportunities to spend time in nature, such as camping, and may choose a profession such as a conservationist, farmer, or botanist.

Existential (Metaphysical)

Existential or metaphysical intelligence deals with understanding ultimate issues. People with strength in this area have a deep understanding of the human condition. They come across as broad-minded people who are open to new ways of working. They like to contemplate abstract concepts. Their curiosity propels them to ask many questions concerning abstract concepts. Religious activities are enjoyable as they find them to be meaningful. Careers in the spiritual life, philosophy, and psychology-related fields serve them well.

* * *

If this seems like more information than you want or need to proceed with the building of exceptional experiences, don't fret. It isn't necessary to overanalyze this information. To simplify this, remember that the knowledge of multiple intelligences is beneficial to be able to identify strengths and weaknesses in yourself and your parents. This tool helps with goal setting as we strive to function by using our strengths, and also know that building up our weaker intelligences is possible and may be needed to obtain a particular goal. As you help your parents realize their unique talents, they gain confidence, which helps them with skill building. For an involved caregiver, this knowledge is valuable.

9

MOVE IT!

To me, if life boils down to one thing, it's movement.
To live is to keep moving.

—Jerry Seinfeld

My physical therapy education involved learning how to move patients. We practiced transferring patients from one surface to another and worked on functional mobility skills such as walking with a cane, getting up off of the floor, and into a car. Part of my education involved learning the techniques of muscle facilitation, which I use to assist my patients to move their extremities and trunk. The goal for the patient is the ability to perform functional activities such as standing up from a chair or walking up a flight of stairs. From my perspective, as a young therapist, if a patient lost a mobility skill, they needed to learn how to move. With practice and feedback from the patient and their body, I soon began to realize that to *learn to move*, they had to *move to learn.*

The act of doing a functional task, such as taking groceries out of a grocery sack, involves mentally planning an activity, the brain sending signals to the muscles required to move the body, and orchestrating all of the movements to create the desired actions and complete the task. During therapy, I am present to use techniques to stimulate my patients' brains and muscles, give verbal feedback on the planning and execution of the activity, and bring awareness to the patients of the movements they perform during activities.

The progress the patients make with their functional activity is much more profound if they perform the actions themselves with awareness. I can see and feel the body responding as well as observe the cognitive processes or thinking skills during the therapeutic activities. As each patient receives input and feedback into their systems, they respond by moving, and finally performing a functional task—and that means new learning is taking place. You can help your parents by giving them feedback as they are doing activities and tasks to bring awareness to their movements and progress.

One of the reasons I chose physical therapy as a profession was because I wanted to help people. When someone needs assistance with a task, we as therapists, mothers, fathers, caregivers, and friends tend to jump in and say, "Let me help you do this." What often happens is the one who wants to help takes over and does the activity for that person. It makes us feel good to help someone and is valuable for *our* brain and body. Unfortunately, it is not always beneficial for the person we're trying to help.

Going overboard to help someone during their therapy worked for me for a time, until I realized I was worn out by the end of the day both physically and mentally. This led to burnout in my job multiple times. Think of a time when you overextended yourself by doing a task for another person or an organization that they should have been able to complete. For example, you may agree to your toddler's request to be carried around during the day long after they have started to walk. This makes your child happy, but at the end of the day, you have an overly dependent child and an aching back.

Although you may enjoy the caregiving role, you have to find the balance between what your parents can do for themselves and how much assistance they need. As your parents use their brain and body to accomplish tasks, they are building and strengthening the circuits in their brains, which enhances their ability to learn and function. Independence with activities is usually the ultimate goal.

To get this point across to my patients, I often tell them my goal is not to connect my brain to their muscles but rather to connect their brain to their muscles. I remind them that my brain is not going home with them and that they need to engage in the therapy process fully with their whole person. Finding a way to get my patient to claim ownership of this proposition is my challenge, and if there is one thing I love, it is a challenge! The above examples are used to help you understand that although you are tempted to assist your loved ones to accomplish activities and exercise, you need to allow them to be active participants in the experience. It would be counterintuitive to the purpose of this book if you were to take over the experiences.

There are two main points I would like to highlight in this chapter. One is that movement and learning pair together. The other is the effect of exercise on the body, brain, and spirit.

MOVEMENT AND LEARNING

If you want to be an active participant in the art of living, you need to be an active participant in learning and movement. To stop learning is to disengage your brain. If you decide to coast through life you may think you are doing fine, but the fact is, there is no such thing as autopilot for your brain. If your brain lacks challenge, it will shrink and the strong neural networks you have built start to weaken and could eventually disappear.[1] Living with a mild amount of tension is good for your brain. This low level of stress keeps the brain awake and stimulated.

As you read this book, you find you are a student of new material and a teacher as you instruct yourself as well as your parents through the process of learning and applying therapeutic encounters. Be aware of the role the body has in learning—or how learning and movement pair together. From the earliest moments we start swimming around in amniotic fluid until we take our last breath, our body plays an essential part in our intellectual functioning. You may be wondering how this happens.

One way movement is involved in learning is that it wakes up the systems and activates the brain. Through bodily movements, the brain is alerted to engage in an activity. The brain is summoned to guide the conscious participation of a response such as to move away from danger, seek pleasure, or finalize a decision.[2] Another way that exercise and movement affect learning is they increase circulation to the brain as well as releasing pleasure chemicals such as serotonin and dopamine that make us feel calm, happy, and euphoric.[3]

Movement of the body aligns us with partaking in sensory experiences, which is vital for learning. For example, think about how young children learn how to feed themselves. They sit in their highchairs playing with food for days to weeks attempting to use their fingers to grasp the food and pick it up. They have learned that to satisfy their hunger, they have to get the food to their mouth, but they have not yet developed the coordination of their hand and arm to get it there. They use their senses and motor control of their body during trial and error until they are successful. Do you remember seeing your child or a picture of a baby with food covering their entire face during this learning period? You can see the effects of trial and error! The movements of the child's body that take place during this process include eye movements back and forth from the food to the hand and then the hand toward the mouth. They also shift their body and move their arm to get the food in their mouth. Moving the body to smell the food, look over at mom's approving smile, and smile at dad while hearing his reassuring voice is also part of learning. This self-feeding movement is repeated many times until it becomes a pattern of movement that is hard-wired in the nervous system through neural pathways. This example demonstrates the point *to learn more, move more.*

Movement is responsible for anchoring new information in our systems.[4] As seen in the example above, by using movement during learning, we can make learning more meaningful as we integrate our physical body, emotional responses, and thinking skills to anchor our thoughts and actions through neural networks.

We continue to build neural networks, or what Carla Hannaford calls base patterns, from our experiences with movement, our senses, emotions, and our previous stores of knowledge. Hannaford says:

> The ultimate artistry comes when we can incorporate all of the base patterning from our knowledge of the world with our senses, emotions, movement, and technical skill—to create something beyond and different from our reality. It is from this place of play, where the integrated brain, rich with base patterns, looks for novel possibilities, that the artistic within us reaches its pinnacle.[5]

This beautifully stated message is referring to an artist creating art. Do you see how it also applies to the art of living? This, my friends, is the expression of art. The artistry of the human being, being human. This is the time when we present ourselves with the freedom to create a new beginning, a change of mind, and a more complex person. I invite you and your parents to accept the challenge of creating yourself.

Movement becomes an expression of our being as we use our bodies to communicate through speaking, writing, gesturing, hugging, making music, and artistic creations. It carries us into our future with everyday experiences that build on each other and finally culminate in the actions we take in all of the roles in our lives. It may be through neurosurgery, parenting, teaching, playing sports, or writing a book.

If we stop moving, we decrease our ability to be creative and live life to the fullest. In fact, movement has a direct effect on creativity. A research study shows that by walking, you can increase your skills of divergent thinking or the creative free flow of ideas.[6] This study also found that walking outdoors produced the most novel and highest quality analogies. When we want to come up with a new idea, solve a problem, or create a piece of music or literature, we should get up on our feet and move, preferably outside! Who doesn't want to be more creative? The fun of life lives in creativity.

This education on how we pair our bodies and brains together for learning is meant to help you and your parents make effective changes for your present and future. It is empowering to know that the brain has the ability for lifelong learning as well as healing. Reorganizing your neural networks in more complex and efficient forms is possible through using your senses and integrated movement. If you value life and learning, you should be moving. The quote at the start of the chapter says it well—to live is to keep moving.

THE EFFECTS OF EXERCISE ON THE BODY, BRAIN, AND SPIRIT

It is a well-known fact that exercise is good for us. We have been told to do aerobic exercises to keep our heart healthy and help us lose weight. If you partake in sports, you know that stretching and strengthening exercises can help you gain an advantage and move you toward success.

Physical activity and exercise offer some serious benefits, which include reducing a person's risk for several conditions including:

- Heart disease
- Diabetes
- Stroke
- High blood pressure
- Depression
- Obesity
- Dementia
- Bone loss
- Falls
- Dependence in later life
- Joint pain

In addition to its crucial preventative role, exercise can also make life better by providing secondary benefits including:

- Improves sleep
- Elevates mood
- Decreases anxiety
- Lessens stress

There are other reasons to partake in the exercises mentioned above, and one relates to the health of your brain. Moderate aerobic exercise has been found to trigger the release of brain-derived neurotrophic factor or BDNF.[7] [8] This natural substance enhances cognition by improving the synaptic transmission, or the neurons' ability to communicate with one another.[9]

Physical exercise training has also been found to increase the size of the portion of the brain called the hippocampus.[10] The hippocampus is responsible for learning and memory.

In his book, *Spark: The Revolutionary New Science of Exercise and the Brain*, Dr. John Ratey explains that BDNF improves the function of neurons, encourages their growth, and strengthens and protects them against the natural process of cell death. It is the crucial biological link between thought, emotions, and movement. Because it is responsible for neurogenesis, or the production of new neural cells, Ratey has dubbed exercise, "Miracle-Gro" for your brain.[11]

Another benefit of exercise is that it increases catecholamines, which are brain chemicals such as norepinephrine, serotonin, and dopamine. They usher in thoughts and emotions and elevate mood.[12]

Exercise has a positive impact on brain health and the ability to think clearly.

Some of the ways it helps your brain include the following:

- Protects memory
- Sharpens cognition
- Increases alertness
- Promotes feelings of well-being
- Increases vitality
- Increases brain volume

Building your brain in your young and middle adulthood is critical and has positive implications as you age. The brain, which has been made strong over the years through the use of exercise, has stored up a reserve of capacities. Experiences that are new and challenging help build up this reserve and slow down mental decline. Overall, *cognitive reserve* allows you to age slower. The good news is, it is never too late to make a difference.

Here are some suggestions on how to build cognitive reserve:

- Apply challenge through mentally stimulating (difficult) activities
- Mix up your exercise routine
- Change your point of view
- Learn a new language
- Explore your strengths and work on your weaknesses
- Take a trip
- Revisit an old hobby or get a new one
- Make time for socialization several times a week

The above recommendations can be included in exceptional experiences for your parents, if appropriate. The critical message is that we need to provide new and stimulating activities to challenge our brains. If we start these practices when we are young, we will be accustomed to including them in our everyday activities as we age. This is valuable information for you and other family members.

Neuroplasticity, or plasticity, is a term we use to describe the brain's ability to form new connections where old ones were lost. "Whenever we engage in new behavior, the brain remodels itself," states Dr. Michael Merzenich.[13] An example of this would be in people who have suffered a stroke and have had an injury to the brain, which results in "death" of the existing neural pathways. As the brain is stimulated through repetition of an exercise with the side of the body that was affected, it forms new pathways to be able to carry out an activity such as lifting your arm. Donald Hebb, a Canadian psychologist, explains this with his theoretical rule that states, "What fires together, wires together."[14] New neural connections are made and the more they fire together due to practice and repetition, the stronger the connection becomes. Because of neuroplasticity, you and your parents have the power to change your brain every day. The good news is that your brains remain plastic, a term used to describe the ability to change, to some degree, even in old age.

Neuroplasticity rewires your brain if you proceed with focused attention, determination, hard work and maintain overall brain health, Merzenich explains in his book, *Soft-Wired: How the New Science of Brain Plasticity Can Change Your Life.*[15] He also states that it is as easy to generate negative changes as it is positive changes in the brain. We have to work hard as we age to avoid the effects of negative wiring on our brains.[16]

There are several ways to work on combatting negative wiring. First, we need to be aware that we are moving in the wrong direction. This can be done through reflection and self-assessment. You can help your parents with this during the exceptional experiences processing time. As they take time to reflect on their experiences, they will note if they are making progress or not. If they or you notice a decline is taking place, identify what is occurring to cause the decline. The next step is taking action to stop the behavior that is promoting the decline. An example of this would be identifying a regression in mobility skills. The action would be to avoid the development of bad habits that may make functional activities and mobility easier but eventually promote a downward spiral into dependency. Work can be done to change the bad habits and positively wire the brain to promote improved mobility and function.

An additional source of negative wiring is when your parents use compensatory behaviors to complete tasks. Instead of using the abilities they have, they find shortcuts to achieve their mental and physical functions. This could include overusing technology and avoiding mental processing. Or, using an electric scooter instead of walking. This negative wiring leads to decline. In other words—if you don't use it, you'll lose it.

Humor is a way to add positivity into your life. Sulking about losses you experience can be turned around by bringing positivity into the present. This can be done with humor and gratitude. Help your parents to stop looking at a situation based on negativity. Making lemonade out of lemons takes training, but it can be done with much practice. Keep repeating the positive behaviors and eventually, they become a habit. Your mind will automatically start seeing the positive aspects of a situation versus the negative ones. Ultimately, we need to believe in ourselves and use a positive approach to carrying out our daily activities and in learning new skills. If you start telling yourself you can do something, your chances of success increase immensely.

Merzenich recommends eight general brain fitness rules to keep your brain in shape and avoid the deterioration that could lead to a very unsatisfying state of life as you age. Some of the rules he explains in his book include finding a new activity to learn that demands your attention and that matters to you. Work on activities that are satisfying and rewarding to you and your brain will want to save them. Find areas to study that provide more complex planning and challenges you as you progress. Track your performance, note even the small advancements, and reward yourself in your mind for your growing achievements. Advance your speed of learning and complexity of the task as you progress.[17]

Internet-delivered brain fitness training demonstrates through positive outcomes of testing that this is a viable source of brain exercise that is making a difference in the cognitive function as well as the functional skills of older adults. One study showed that brain training focusing on aural speech listening very significantly improves memory and other cognitive abilities, and results in substantial improvement recorded by brain speed and accuracy.[18] Another study promotes the benefits of using brain training exercises to help people improve their daily living skills.[19] Improving cognitive abilities and independence with daily tasks helps your parents age in place and enjoy their aging years.

Integrate these principles of brain training into your parents' life, using the exceptional experiences you build, as they learn new hobbies, functional skills, games, sports, and take part in sensory experiences. Brain training exercises that are computer-based are an excellent activity to add to your parents' day. Help your parents choose to embrace life with excitement and new learning. This will ultimately bring them the joy and fulfillment they can spread to others.

AN EXERCISE PRESCRIPTION

This book uses exercise and movement as a strategy, or tool, in the therapeutic experience process. General information is provided below for the recommended exercises. However, keep in mind that a specific prescription for an exercise program should be tailored and designed for each person based on their particular needs. Work with your parents' doctors and therapists to receive individualized instruction as needed. It helps to teach your parents to use their judgment to work within the guidelines the professionals provide.

Stretching—Keeping muscles at their optimal length helps with balance and mobility skills. It also helps to decrease the risk of falls. Your parents need functional motion in their spine, arms, and legs to do the activities of daily living such as getting dressed, transferring in and out of bed, and continuing their exercises and hobbies.

Your parents can stretch their muscles by taking their arms, legs, spine, and head through the motions of bending forward and backward, side to side and rotation if the joint allows, within their comfort level. Stretching by reaching and bending done during normal daily activities is an excellent way to stretch safely.

Do not force or overstretch a muscle or joint as this can cause damage. Just remember, if it's not broken, don't fix it. In other words, don't try to achieve the normal range-of-motion if you haven't had it for years and are doing fine with your functional activities in your current range. By taking the arms, legs, and spine to the comfortable end range-of-motion and holding it for 20 seconds, five times each, your parents can gain motion slowly. Consult with professionals if your parents need extra guidance with stretching exercises. Daily stretching for brief periods is encouraged. See the endnotes for a resource on stretching.[20]

Strengthening—To build strength in muscles, you need to provide resistance. You can get resistance by applying weights, using stretchy bands for exercising or using your body weight as resistance.

The golden rule, so to speak, for strengthening is that the muscle should be fatigued at the end of 10 repetitions of an exercise. If your muscle is not tired at the end of 10 repetitions, then add weights. Start with one pound and add weights as tolerated. Do 2 sets of 10 repetitions for each exercise. An arthritic joint may not tolerate weight training. The pressure of weights can cause arthritic joints to flare up with inflammation and pain. An alternative exercise for arthritic joints is isometric exercises where the muscle is contracted but the joint does not move. Exercises in a pool of water are also easy on the joints and more tolerable for people with arthritis.

For those who have good balance and some personal assistance, I like using the Swiss ball for exercise. They are inexpensive and help build trunk or core muscle strength. The core of the body needs to be strong to protect the spine and to give your parents stability during the activities of daily living. Purchase a Swiss ball that is the size corresponding to your parent's height. There are directions on the side of the box to give you this information.

The best way to get a customized exercise program is to seek professional advice from a physical or occupational therapist. Some people hire personal trainers that come into the home or meet you at the gym to help you get started and progress on an exercise program.

Work on strengthening exercises three times a week. Let your muscles rest on their days off or choose another type of exercise or activity. See endnotes for a recommended website that provide detailed instructions to get started.[21]

Therapeutic Activity—This is another effective way to use exercise to gain muscle strength, range of motion, activity tolerance, and balance. Gardening, dancing, cleaning your home, cooking a meal, and other forms of activity-producing hobbies are great ways to add exercise to your parents' day. Ballroom dancing is a combination of mental and physical exercise which boosts brain health by challenging the brain using coordination, rhythm, and strategy. This type of exercise is beneficial for a total body/brain workout. When choosing activities, keep in mind that brains and bodies love dancing!

Aerobic Exercise—This exercise elevates your heart rate and is essential for heart and brain health. Aerobic exercise should be done for 30 minutes, three to five times a week, at the target heart rate to ensure the benefits for the body and brain. For your parents, this could include taking the stairs several times a day, walking an extra block, or participating in a standing exercise group session. There are videos for seniors for home use if you need assistance.

Your parents' heart rate should be 60-80% of their maximum heart rate during the aerobic exercise session. This is called their target heart rate. They should start at a lower level and increase their heart rate as tolerated.

You can find their maximum heart rate by subtracting their age from 220. If they are 70 years old, their maximum heart rate would be 150 bpm (beats per minute). Their target heart rate at a low level of 50% would be 75 bpm, and at a high level of 85% would be 127 bpm.

They can monitor their heart rate with a heart rate monitor or by taking their pulse. Find their pulse on the thumb side of their inner wrist. Count the pulse for six seconds and add a zero to find the beats per minute. There is a chart below you can use to calculate target heart rates.

Another way to measure if their heart rate is adequate for moderate aerobic exercise is to have them talk while they exercise. They should take breaths every three to four words during their exercise routine if they are working at their target heart rate. Or they should be able to talk, but not sing. See endnotes for additional aerobic exercise recommendations for seniors.[22]

AEROBIC HEART RATE CHART				
AGE	MAXIMUM HR	50 PERCENT	75 PERCENT	85 PERCENT
40	180	90	135	153
45	175	88	131	149
50	170	85	127	144
55	165	83	123	140
60	160	80	120	136
65	155	78	116	132
70	150	75	113	127
75	145	72	108	123
80	140	70	104	119
85	135	68	101	115

Figure 9.1

Brain Exercises—There are brain exercises that you can access through the internet, find in books, or develop yourself through challenging therapeutic activities. There is a list below of brain functions that can be addressed. Access more information about each category via brain training websites where leaders in the field discuss in detail how each function is trained.

There are daily activities you can participate in to get started. For instance, to improve your memory, challenge yourself to remember the names of people you just met. Or, write down the groceries you want to buy and then put the list away when you are in the store and try to remember as many items as you can off of the list. Learn some new words of a foreign language and use them during the week. Pick out a new coffee shop across town, map out the directions in your mind, and write them down. See if your directions work to get you to your destination. Put together a jigsaw puzzle. The ideas are endless.

Brain training can help you maintain your current status of cognitive functioning, increase your function to be able to excel and function at your highest level or help you in recovery from a neurological condition such as a stroke.

Brain exercises include but are not limited to the following:

- Memory
- Attention
- Language
- Visual-spatial
- Executive function
- Accuracy
- Brain speed
- Navigation in time and space
- People skills
- Flexible intelligence

These exercises can be a part of your parents' daily therapeutic experiences. You and your parents can make a plan that utilizes the resources they have available to them to make this a reality. Build your therapeutic experiences to include stretching and brain exercises daily, strengthening and aerobic exercises three times a week, and therapeutic activities can be done daily. Build up tolerance to exercises slowly.

The movement your parents partake in could be anything from ballroom or belly dancing to being pushed around in a wheelchair. Each action has its place in time. Whatever the activity is, note the movements, feel the muscle contractions, and think about what you are doing for your body and brain. If you have not started this process, now is the time to begin. Nike said it well with their slogan, *Just do it.* I might add, *Just don't do it for them.* Or at least let them do as much as they can for themselves.

10

EXPERIENTIAL LEARNING

Education is the single most important job of the
human race.

—George Lucas

We have seen how compelling experiences can be in our lives. They provide sensory input, prepare us to learn, and teach new concepts and skills. There is a theory on learning, based on experiences, that will help you build education into your exceptional experiences.

In 1984, American educational theorist, David A. Kolb, developed a learning theory based on involving the acquisition of abstract concepts that can be applied flexibly in a range of situations. He states, "Learning is the process whereby knowledge is created through the transformation of experience."[1]

In simpler terms, what his theory proposes is that we learn best through experience and reflection. How does Kolb propose we do this? He demonstrates through his research that acquiring competence is a continuous process of experience, reflection, conceptualization, and experimentation. He set up a cyclical model of learning based on the relationship between the four stages.

Kolb's Experiential Learning Cycle

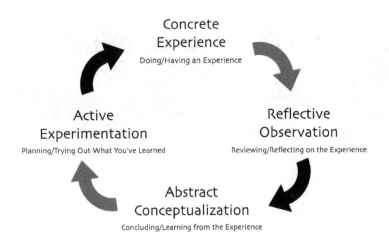

Figure 10.1

Let's take learning how to ride a bicycle as an example of new learning as we travel through the Experiential Learning Cycle.

CONCRETE EXPERIENCE

The first stage, concrete experience, involves actively participating in an unfamiliar activity, encountering a new experience or situation, or having a reinterpretation of an existing experience. In order to learn how to ride a bike, you have to get on the bike and have the experience. It doesn't take long to figure out if you are successful! During this first step of having the experience, we learn by trial and error—which includes our mistakes as well as achievements.

REFLECTIVE OBSERVATION

During the stage of reflective observation, there is a period to consciously reflect on the experience. It is a time to ponder over the experience, determine what went right or wrong, and learn from others. This is also a time to compare the current experience to past experiences and determine how to accept or change them. Research confirms that quality reflection time is vital for learning.[2] As you think of your experience on the bike, you realize your success and failure. For instance, you may note that you were able to ride for 20 feet but you kept falling to the left, your wheels weren't lined up, and you were moving too slow.

ABSTRACT CONCEPTUALIZATION

The third stage is abstract conceptualization, where you work to conceptualize a theory or model of what is observed in relation to what you already know. The reflection gives rise to a new idea or modification to an existing concept. This is the time for brainstorming and planning abstract concepts and strategies for success. You think of other ways to be successful at riding a bike such as keeping the tires lined up through steering, shifting your weight to the right to keep balanced, and peddling faster.

ACTIVE EXPERIMENTATION

The fourth stage, active experimentation, is the time you take a plan of action and test it in the real world. This is where everything comes together, and you can implement a concept through daily experiences—and see results. Now you are ready to get back on the bike and practice all of the strategies you designed to achieve success—and you ride off into the sunset!

From this success, further learning occurs as concepts and ideas are used for future experiences, resulting in new learning. This cycle continues and is a way to build our knowledge base, which helps us develop new habits and behaviors.

You can see from the diagram that the stages, one through four, consist of doing, observing, thinking, and planning. Use these words to describe the stages to your parents during new learning activities. This brings awareness to the stage of learning and encourages your parent to be an active learner. Start the learning experience at any of the four stages but know that effective learning occurs only when a person can execute all four stages of the model. No one stage can be singled out as a learning procedure.

Kolb also describes four distinct *learning styles* based on his four-stage learning cycle. According to his theory, a preferred learning style could be influenced by educational experiences, a social environment, or the basic cognitive structure of the individual.[3]

The four learning styles include the following:

1. **Assimilators** are those who learn better when they are given a good, clear explanation rather than a practical opportunity. They prefer to think and watch.
2. **Convergers** appreciate practical applications of concepts and theories to help them learn. They thrive on the use of technical tasks to find ways to solve problems by experimenting with new ideas and work toward practical applications. They like to think and do.
3. **Accommodators** prefer to participate in "hands-on" experiences to learn more efficiently. They rely more on their intuition rather than logic. They look to other people for information and then use an experimental approach through feeling and doing.

4. **Divergers** observe and collect a wide range of information and then apply it to their learning techniques. They are sensitive and use their imagination to solve problems from feeling and watching.

Your parents may identify with one or two learning styles they prefer to use during learning experiences. As with any theory, there are mixed reviews and opinions on whether learning styles make a difference in learning. In your case, it may help to think about whether you can use this information to work more effectively with your parents.

AN EXAMPLE OF EXPERIENTIAL LEARNING

Let's look at another real-life situation and track the progression of learning. Exercising on the Swiss ball is an event that involves new learning for most of the geriatric population. If you are not familiar with this piece of exercise equipment, it is a large ball that you use for exercises mainly for strengthening your core or trunk muscles. I use one to sit on instead of a desk chair, and they can be found in most gyms. This is one of my favorite forms of learning because it involves the brain receiving feedback from the muscles, joints, visual, and vestibular system. The vestibular system is located in the inner ear and is responsible for your balance.

Many patients are reluctant to use the Swiss ball for exercise as it appears to be challenging and elicits insecurity and fear. I attempt to decrease the patient's anxiety by sitting on the Swiss ball and demonstrating the exercises. As I sit on the ball with my feet firmly planted in a wide base of support, I move the ball forward and backward, side to side, clockwise, and counterclockwise, explaining the progression of exercises. I am looking for their reaction and assessment of the activity. Some are very willing to participate, and others need the reassurance that I will be holding onto the gait belt around their waist and sitting on a stool behind them to guard them against falling. Most are then willing to try the exercises. This activity of demonstrating the exercise is a chance for the patient to learn from others, compare this exercise to others they have done in the past, and start forming abstract concepts about how to move their body once they are sitting on the Swiss ball. They are in Stage Three of the learning cycle.

After they sit on the Swiss ball with my assistance, they are guided to achieve their balance. I can see and feel them going through the first stage of Kolb's theory, and that is "doing." They move a little on the ball and receive feedback from their sensory systems. Most people stay in their comfort zone, over their center of gravity, and within their base of support. In other words, they aren't too adventurous! After they gain confidence in their abilities, they can be more courageous with the exercises and start to move outside of their base of support, which means moving their upper body away from the center. I hold onto the gait belt and help them feel secure and balanced while gradually guiding them into more challenging exercises. They may need extra assistance from another person or a sturdy rail to hold onto to feel secure.

The goal of this exercise is to sit up on the ball and not lose balance. During this process of concrete experience, their brain receives information from the systems and then sends out messages to the arms, legs, and trunk to move as needed to keep them upright and balanced. If the brain does not get sufficient input—or cannot respond to the information—they will have difficulty adjusting their body and could continue to lose balance, especially as the exercises increase in complexity. They may ask to quit the activity or end up with their feet off the floor, needing assistance from the therapists. I continue to assist the patient with verbal cues and physical assistance so they can experience this stage as long as the patient is comfortable with the process. Stage One is accomplished if the patient can experience the Swiss ball exercise in any amount.

Two scenarios could follow. The first one is that they start moving through the learning cycle during the activity. They observe and reflect on their body movements, think of how to make adjustments to keep their balance, and finally put that plan into action to balance on the Swiss ball and start advanced exercises and activities. They may have developed abstract concepts about how to balance on the Swiss ball so that when we bounce a ball to them, they can reach out of their base of support to catch it and throw it back, all while keeping their balance. They may then experiment with a planned activity for another exercise while on the Swiss ball and I can pick up on their learning progression as they have reached Stage Four, or active experimentation. They have traveled through the complete learning cycle and now can take a break and continue to reflect on their experience and do additional abstract planning for the next time they try it. Or, they can use this experience to assist them in succeeding in other functional skills they need to work on.

The second scenario is that they cannot transition to Stage Two of reflective observance during the activity. This is apparent if someone needs total assistance to sit on the ball to maintain their balance. Some patients even roll backward and have no contact with the floor. I'm always prepared for a surprise! In that case, we do as much as we can in Stage One to be able to achieve balance with good posture, their body in midline, and feet contacting the floor. This gives their body and brain input to know what is expected of them to be able to sit on the ball and exercise.

After we obtain a well-rounded experience, we assist them off of the Swiss ball and the period of reflection starts. I ask them questions about their experience to help them start thinking about what changes they will make to achieve success the next time they attempt this exercise. They will need time to reflect and possibly even observe someone else exercising on the Swiss ball and then they can proceed to plan strategies for success. Experimenting may take place the next few times they exercise on the Swiss ball. It is impressive to see that most people find exceptional results in a few days to weeks of experiential learning on the Swiss ball.

The above scenario is an excellent example of neuroplasticity. The brain and body are challenged through a new exercise experience, forming new neural networks, which over time promotes advanced learning. Increased practice with the exercise increases the strength of the neural networks, which will then become ingrained in the knowledge base. This knowledge can then be used for other activities they need in their daily lives such as balance for walking on uneven surfaces or weight shifting to reach up into a cupboard.

The individuals who have a continual loss of balance during Stage One may feel like their time on the Swiss ball was a complete waste of time. In reality, if that step does not occur, an important part of the experiential learning experience is absent. The doing portion has to take place in the cycle. At times I decide that this exercise is too much of a leap forward for the patient. I downgrade the exercise and meet my patient at their mental and physical level. I find other exercises to challenge them that provide kinesthetic awareness before attempting therapy on the Swiss ball again.

Anxiety can affect how long it takes someone to adjust to this activity, especially if the person has suffered a recent fall. It helps if the person is alert, focused, and aware of what purpose the activity has in their life. It may appear as if success did not happen during the treatment that day, but we typically find that the body and brain have responded and we are making progress toward our end goals. I never view feeding the brain with helpful information as wasted time.

Your parents benefit from exercises that promote muscle strength and balance as well as from learning new skills they will need to age successfully. Knowing the progression of learning gives you and your parents a reference point to help you as you plan activities and therapeutic experiences. Complete the form below using an example from your past or present to better understand how each of these steps plays a role in learning.

My experience is _____

Stage One: The experience entailed _____

_____

Stage Two: Write down your observations about what was successful and what was not as you reflect on this experience.

_____

_____

Stage Three: Apply what you learned to your knowledge base and brainstorm new ideas, plans, and strategies for success.

_____

_____

Stage Four: Name the practice points, experimentations, or repetitions you used to test this experience in real life situations.

_____

_____

As you reflect on this educational experience in your own life, you can further learn how to apply experiential learning to therapeutic encounters for your loved ones to meet their needs. When you develop therapeutic encounters, keep in mind that a visual demonstration of the activity can be your key to success. Older individuals depend more strongly on mental practice for the acquisition of motor memory.[4] I have worked with many people who struggle with learning functional mobility activities until they see a visual demonstration, and then they *get it*.

Don't shy away from giving the right amount of challenge during the learning process. There are many times when I ask patients to practice balance by standing on a piece of dense foam while holding onto a stable surface or rail. I am assisting the patient to maintain balance during the exercises. The first session can be challenging. It's common for a patient to complain that the exercise is too hard. I reassure the patient that after a couple of weeks practicing, it is much easier to stand on one leg and in a heel-to-toe stance. The progress measured at each session is relayed to the patient so they can track their progress. This motivates them to push themselves to achieve more. The patient is encouraged as it becomes apparent to them that strength and balance can improve with exercise. It will be evident during the learning episodes if they already possess a skill or if they need time in the Experiential Learning Cycle for doing, reflection, thinking, and planning.

11

JUST BREATHE, EAT, DRINK, MEDITATE, AND SLEEP

Prevention is better than cure.

—Desiderius Erasmus

Your mother and grandmother were right when they told you to relax, take a deep breath, drink plenty of water, don't eat junk food, get a good night's sleep, and meditate or say your prayers. What they appeared to know instinctively about these practices is being extensively researched, and the results reveal that following their advice has life-changing and life-saving benefits.

As we attempt to follow this guidance, we are likely to find ourselves doing reasonably well until our lives become too fast-paced. We are then pressed to find short-cuts to perform these necessary activities. This leads to poor diets, shallow breathing, a few hours of restless sleep every night, and not enough time to reflect and meditate. We miss out on the benefits of feeling good, being productive, and taking care of our bodies and brains. As a result, we set ourselves up for potentially contracting a host of chronic diseases. Choices can be made to reduce or eliminate the risk of poor health as we treat our body to options that are good for us.

At this time in history, we have at our fingertips—via the internet, books, and webinars—cutting-edge methods for healthy living based on years of research. I will teach you some of the basics so you can help your parents make lifestyle changes that can significantly impact their health. You can investigate the five essential items in this chapter, learn how to do them well, and apply them to you and your parents' everyday life. Reaching an optimal state of health opens the door to achieving the dreams and desires we carry through our lives. This book provides information to help you take steps to implement this process of health and well-being.

BREATHE

Breathing seems to be a simple function: inhale...exhale...inhale...exhale. At times when you are relaxed and calm, your breathing is normal. However, when you find yourself anxious, overworked, multi-tasking, or not living in the present moment, your breathing may be shallow, or you might find yourself holding your breath.

Due to lung disease, dysfunction, and during periods when we do not breathe correctly, our blood's oxygen level may drop. This desaturation of oxygen in the blood may be harmful to our vital organs. This is because we rely on oxygen to break down food through a process called oxidation. Your brain and body receive this energy, supplied by oxidation, as fuel to keep them functioning. The brain requires one-fifth of the body's oxygen.[1] It is so vital for your body and mind that death occurs within minutes of not receiving this life-giving element.

Becoming aware of your breath as you would other parts of your life such as your diet or level of exercise is a part of healthy living. Breathwork, or breathing exercises, provides healing to your body and brain as they can calm you down, promote relaxation, and switch off your fight or flight nervous system response.

Diaphragmatic breathing, sometimes called belly breathing, is a technique used to promote deep breathing. This can allow for an increased amount of oxygen to enter your lungs. Your diaphragm is a muscle that sits just below your lungs. As it contracts, it moves in a downward direction and allows for more room to expand your lungs. As it relaxes, it returns to your chest area and assists you in pushing the air out of your lungs as they deflate.

You can practice this breathing technique by getting into a relaxed position, either sitting or lying down. After you learn this technique well, you can also do it standing. Make sure your back is straight, and your shoulders are back. Place one hand on each side of your lower ribcage and outer abdomen. Imagine sandbags are weighing your shoulders down. Now, clear your mind of the busy thoughts running through it.

Breathe through your nose. As you inhale, the hands on your ribcage area should move outward, and you should feel the lower part of your rib cage expand—similar to an umbrella opening up. As you exhale, your rib cage and abdomen return to a relaxed position. Practice this exercise 5 to 10 minutes, twice a day. If you start to feel lightheaded, stop the exercise, make sure you are sitting down, and wait until your head clears. As your body learns this method of calm breathing, you should see a habit start to form. Increase your practice time to five to ten minutes, three to four times a day. This breathing technique is especially useful when you are feeling stress, attempting to calm yourself down, and need to manage pain.

Dr. Andrew Weil recommends the breathing exercise below for relaxation.[2] Find a comfortable place to sit or lie down. Prepare to start the exercise by resting the tip of your tongue on the roof of your mouth, just behind your front teeth. Keep your tongue in place throughout the entire exercise.

1. Exhale completely through your mouth, making a whoosh sound.
2. Close your mouth and inhale quietly through your nose to a mental count of **four**.
3. Hold your breath for a count of **seven**.
4. Exhale completely through your mouth through slightly pursed lips, making a whoosh sound to a count of **eight**.
5. This is one breath. Now inhale again and repeat the cycle three more times for a total of four breaths.

Practice this for four breaths, two times a day for one month. You can then work up to eight breaths, two times a day. This promotes overall health and wellness.

Teaching my patients how to breathe is one of the most useful, life-changing therapy tools I give them—and it's a simple way you can help your parents. It can be challenging to learn this exercise if upper chest breathing was practiced for years. Shortness of air caused by chronic lung disease causes anxiety, which leads to more dysfunctional breathing. This habit of shallow breathing does not serve a person well. I continue to educate people struggling with this condition by giving them opportunities to practice diaphragmatic breathing in the comfort of their home with a home exercise program and the use of relaxing music, meditation, and visualization.

One way to bring attention to breathing while you are with your parents is to start talking about it. See what their response is. Ask them if they are interested in learning a breathing technique to improve their health. Explain the importance of breathing well. Practice diaphragmatic breathing together if your parent agrees. There are professionals such as physical, occupational, and respiratory therapists who teach this method of breathing. Consult a doctor for a referral to these professionals if your parent is having difficulty breathing or is short of breath with minor exertion.

Finding an activity that clears your parents' mind of excess worry, relaxes their body, and brings about peace may naturally help them practice a form of deeper breathing. This might include hobbies like fishing, nature walks, or bird watching. Setting up a relaxing environment at home with lights dimmed, classical music, and a comfortable place to sit or lie down can also be helpful.

The breath work that I practice involves the use of relaxation, visualization, and meditation. This is something I teach my patients as it takes some of the focus off of the mechanics of breathing exercises. When I use these techniques, I notice that my breathing naturally becomes deeper and slower, and I genuinely feel the relaxation I'm working toward with less physical effort. I will give more information on visualization in the meditation section below.

You will see that as you turn your attention to breathing, you may find yourself starting to meditate and begin mindful living, which in turn, will bring slower, deeper breathing. This becomes a cycle you can use for relaxation. Take time to practice the art of breathing with your parents.

NUTRITION

Healthy nutrition is not a complicated concept, but getting your parents to make a change in their diet may take some time and effort. The education provided below equips you with enough knowledge to get started on helping them make changes with food choices and diet. Before you start clearing their refrigerator and pantry of any unhealthy food and dictating a specific diet to them, it would be wise to teach them some interesting facts that may do the persuading for you.

Research has proven that healthy diets and lifestyle choices starting at a young age and continuing throughout one's life can have a positive effect on heart health and longevity. Current studies also demonstrate that what is good for the body is also good for the brain. Dietary choices made to fuel the brain and decrease inflammation have profound effects on health.

We now have more information on processed foods that are harming our bodies and brains. A change in diet to include the healthy foods our body needs and take away those that are causing dysfunction in our systems is a remarkable way to improve health. Start with the baseline of your parents' current diet and from there, plan the changes that make you both comfortable. Little changes adhered to consistently can make a big difference in the long run.

Diet is a very personal preference for most individuals. We have attachments to particular foods we know are not good for us, but don't want to give up. Moderation is a good rule to follow. One way to practice moderation is to use is the 80/20 rule, meaning 80% of the food you eat is healthy and 20% is not as healthy. After you master this, move to the 90/10 rule. Healthy eating then reaches the 90% level. This gives you a chance to indulge in a favorite snack or treat that may not make the healthy list, a few times a week.

Overeating is prevalent in our society. We take in too many calories, or even empty calories that do not provide any nutritional benefit. Cut down on portion size, limit desserts, and replace food full of sugar and fat with fresh fruits and vegetables to give your body a chance to function in the way it was made to work—and see some fantastic results in your health and weight.

Your parents will most likely need some guidance with their diet as they age. Their appetites could decrease due to their diminishing sense of smell. Not being hungry or interested in food could lead to not purchasing nutritious food or making poor food choices during the day. If your parent has difficulty chewing food, there are healthy options with minimal sugar in the form of liquid shakes they can drink.

A good rule to live by is to eat whole and natural foods as much as possible. If your food comes in a package and has more than one item in the list of ingredients, be cautious. Processed food is a food item that has had various mechanical or chemical manipulations performed on it to change or preserve it. Our bodies recognize and accept whole, natural foods.

Foods to eliminate from your diet include the following:

- Processed sugar
- Processed flour
- Fast food
- Processed food
- Saturated fats and hydrogenated oils

Foods to eat for optimal health include the following:

- Fruits
- Beans and legumes
- Vegetables, especially leafy greens
- Fish with Omega 3 such as salmon or sablefish, twice a week
- Grass-fed beef—limit red meat
- Fats from olive oil, coconut oil, and avocados instead of butter
- Whole grains
- Nuts such as almonds, cashews, pistachios, and walnuts
- Moderate intake of low-fat dairy options
- Season meals with herbs and spices instead of salt
- A daily glass of wine, if you choose

The Mediterranean diet has been shown to promote longer, healthier lives.[3] It follows the above guidelines and also has a social aspect to it as it recommends dining with others and participating in exercise. Many people refer to this as a lifestyle, not a diet. This diet is known to have the elements that feed and protect your body and brain.[4] It works to provide omega-3 fatty acids, antioxidant nutrients, and phytochemicals—especially resveratrol. In addition to those, it supplies the B vitamins and folate that are also important for cognitive or brain function.[5] There are a wide variety of books along with websites for additional details of the Mediterranean diet. Mayo Clinic has information along with a pyramid to give you guidelines for the balance of the above elements. They also provide information on stretching a budget, making good food choices, and healthy recipes. They cite studies that support following the Mediterranean diet to reduce rates of cancer, Parkinson's, and Alzheimer's disease.[6]

In addition to a healthy diet, you can supplement with vitamins, minerals, and other key elements that are vital for the body and brain. I believe we will continue to see a shift toward the intake of healthy food and the detoxification of the chemicals and metals, which are harming our bodies and brains. As you help your parents get started on this path to eating well, think about helping them make good food choices, follow one or two informational sources such as websites or books about healthy nutrition, and work toward the 80/20 rule.

HYDRATION

In addition to what we eat, what we drink is vital for good health. One essential fluid is good, clean water. Our brains and muscles cannot function without it. If we are asking our parents to be secure in their mobility and cognitive skills, we have to equip them with the right fuel. To keep their systems balanced and functioning at an optimal level, they need to be hydrated. Dehydration, or the lack of fluid, can cause an imbalance in the body that could lead to blood clots, seizures, and other medical complications that could be fatal. Be aware of chemicals called diuretics, which dehydrate the body. They are present in alcohol, caffeine, chocolate, and some carbonated beverages. Your parents should have a glass of water within reach during the day, and if they go outside for and activity, take a bottle of water.

The benefits of drinking enough water include the following:

- Keeping body temperature within a normal range
- Lubricating and cushioning joints
- Protecting the spine and other tissues
- Eliminating waste through sweat, urine, and bowel movements
- Maintaining electrolyte (sodium) balance
- Normalizing blood pressure
- Stabilizing the heartbeat

Dehydration can lead to serious problems including the following:

- Confusion or unclear thinking
- Fatigue
- Mood changes
- Overheating
- Kidney stone formation
- Shock

The recommended water intake for women over 19 years old is 2.7 liters (91 fluid ounces) and for men over 19 years old is 3.7 liters (125 fluid ounces).[7] Water intake is dependent on how much fluid you are receiving from food such as fruits and vegetables every day as well as how much exercise you are doing in a day. You may have to increase or decrease water consumption per your daily routine. An excellent visual cue to know if you are hydrated is your urine should be light yellow.

MEDITATION, MINDFULNESS, AND PRAYER

Meditation is a habitual process used to train your mind to focus and to redirect your thoughts.[8]

It is a simple practice that can be done anywhere, anytime, and takes no special equipment. Many people find that it reduces stress, brings about self-awareness, and increases concentration.[9]

Older people and those suffering from neurodegenerative diseases who used meditation techniques benefitted as there was a positive effect in the areas of attention, memory, verbal fluency, and cognitive flexibility.[10] Meditation can be an effective non-pharmacological intervention to prevent cognitive decline in the elderly.[11] Another health benefit of meditation is decreasing the inflammation response caused by stress.[12] This inflammation is linked to many chronic diseases.

Meditation is a practice of clearing the mind. To start meditating, sit or lie down in a quiet and comfortable setting. Set a timer for two minutes if you are a beginner. Close your eyes. Breathe naturally. Do not try to control your breath. Focus your attention on your breath. Note how your body moves as you breathe. If your mind starts to wander, bring it back to the awareness of your breath. Practice this for two to three minutes and increase your time when you feel confident.

Visualization during meditation is a technique that works for me. I am able to enter a deep state of relaxation and breathing. The visualization I use and teach includes taking the mind to a peaceful place. A location where I have vacationed such as a southern beach or the Wisconsin woods near Lake Superior are some of the most physically and mentally relaxing times I have experienced. I place that picture in my head as I let go of my thoughts, clear my mind, and let my body relax.

As I visualize the setting of a peaceful time, my breathing changes naturally. I feel my lower rib cage expand as my lungs fill with air. When my body reaches this relaxed state, my thoughts often go back to my childhood. A feeling of security and peace envelops me. My awareness shifts to the expansion of my lungs.

I start to feel a heaviness in my muscles as they relax, and my mind is drawn to this awareness. I can sense changes in the state of my body, which further relaxes me. I then focus on the feelings deep inside my muscles. If a thought runs through my head, I take note and then let it pass.

I attempt to stay in this state as long as I can and notice the changes my body is experiencing. My muscle tension decreases, my posture improves, my skin tone changes, and my facial expression relaxes. This state is a sharp contrast to how my body reacts to anxiety and stress with shallow upper chest breathing, tightened muscles, and a furrowed brow.

There are many different types of meditation. Try a few of them and select the ones that are working for you and your parents.

Mindfulness is a practice of developing awareness through paying attention to the unfolding of an ongoing experience in the present moment. It is a way of living that involves purpose and non-judgment during the activity. Mindfulness is a form of meditation.

A study using an eight-week program of Mindfulness-Based Stress Reduction (MBSR) found that participants had significant improvements in cognitive function and functional improvements in everyday activities. This means mindfulness training could be a good option for therapeutic intervention for people with mild cognitive impairment.[13]

The loss of volume of the hippocampus, located deep in the brain, is one of the earliest reliable indicators of Mild Cognitive Impairment and Alzheimer's Disease.[14] Mindfulness positively affects the growth of several brain structures, including the hippocampus.[15] Another positive study concluded that by practicing mindfulness, there was a decrease in brain cell volume in the amygdala, which is responsible for fear, anxiety, and stress.[16]

The preliminary results from studies show that the practice of long-term mindfulness has a positive effect on those who have mild cognitive impairments in their ability to improve cognitive function and participate in activities of daily living.[17] That means mindfulness training can be a tool to help your parents increase their thinking skills and participate in daily activities with less assistance—which decreases the burden of care on the support person and family.

The benefits of meditation and mindfulness include the following:

- Reduces stress
- Controls anxiety and social anxiety disorder
- Increases attention span and concentration
- May reduce age-related memory loss
- Promotes emotional health
- Enhances self-awareness
- Helps with addiction
- Generates kindness
- Improves sleep
- Helps control pain
- Increases performance
- Decreases blood pressure

To practice mindfulness, turn your awareness to the activity you are performing. Use all of your senses to take in the sensory experiences you are having right now, during the action. If you are doing dishes, feel the temperature of the water, watch the water and soap bubbles flow over the plates, note the feeling of placing the dishes in the rack to dry. Do not think of the tension you felt yesterday as dwelling on the past tends to cause depression. Do not think of the unknowns of the future as we don't know what it holds, and negative thinking causes anxiety. Participate in the present moment without judgment. Notice how, in this period of awareness, you feel space. Try a guided meditation for resting in the flow which is found in the endnotes.[18]

Prayer is a form of reaching outside of yourself to a higher being to ask for intercessions, forgiveness, or to praise, in most religions. Some believe that prayer is similar to meditation, as prayer is usually done in a meditative mood. Eastern meditation is usually based on clearing the mind of thoughts. Prayer is a practice that fills the mind with a thought, for example, during contemplative prayer the mind is cleared and a thought is contemplated.

Prayer is a personal practice. There are health benefits associated with prayer, including relaxation and deep breathing experienced while praying. For some, prayer adds balance to their life in a spiritual realm. I practice prayer daily and consider it an experience.

How will meditation, mindfulness, and prayer help your parents? As your parents age, they will face new challenges that will require them to be present in the moment, for instance, when they need to learn a new skill or sharpen an existing skill. As you read above, mindfulness helps increase the size of the hippocampus in the brain, which is responsible for learning and memory.

Other benefits include decreased anxiety, improved mood, and lower levels of stress. Stress management is one of the most important things we can do for our health and the health of our parents. The negative impact of chronic stress on health ranges from decreasing immunity to minor illnesses, such as the common cold, and causing an overreactive immune system resulting in autoimmune diseases.[19] Experiencing stress even makes it likely a person will develop cardiovascular disease.[20]

This paragraph makes me want to stop to breathe and meditate. Be gone, stress!

With all of the stress we encounter, we seem to be losing the art of enjoying living in the moment. What interests me is that I think most people don't mind this, or we are getting used to it. Do you ever see a group of people engaged in each other's company, laughing, and making a deep emotional connection, and wish that was you?

We have experienced significant changes in our lives in the last few years, especially with the advancements of technology and the internet. Although we may feel more wired together by social media, we are far less connected. We can't turn back, but we can do something to protect ourselves, so we do not lose what is most precious to us: our brain. I am so happy to see there is a movement taking shape in our culture to teach people how to be mindful and how to meditate.

There are so many things going on that distract us from mindful living. Much of this is due to the technology that provides information and social media. The technology can be convenient at times, and I am grateful for it as I write this book. However, it does make me long for the past, as day after day, I encounter so many people in relationships with *something* instead of someone.

I know I am slow on the uptake of this new way of life. When I ask friends for the location of the restaurant we are going to, they look at me like I must be joking, reach for their phone, and promptly give me the address. They have missed the point that what I'm looking for is engagement, a conversation about an interesting area of town, and mapping it out in my brain versus looking at a map on my phone. I suppose I should make my needs known, but telling my friends that I'm trying to increase the size of my hippocampus may sound weird![21] It appears we have different needs—one is to engage, and the other is to find an answer. Both are valid options, and many days I'm the one looking for an answer.

We receive information so quickly from the multitude of resources we have access to that it appears to me at times we find the answer, shut our brains off, and stop there. Our minds are full of all kinds of information, some relevant and some useless. Are we taking the time to reflect on the meaningful material and do something with it?

I recently stumbled upon a TEDxTeen talk that opened my mind up to an interesting proposition. A young person and genius, Jacob Barnett, who also has autism, advises all of us who want to solve a problem: stop learning, start thinking, begin creating, and solve a problem.[22] He gave examples of the famous scientists Isaac Newton and Albert Einstein who had to stop formal education due to the plague that shut down a university and rejection by a university, respectively. They each had approximately two years to spend time doing one thing—thinking. The theories of relativity and gravity were discovered during their time away from formal education.

When was the last time you were extremely interested in a subject and became intently focused on learning about it? After you learned as much as you could, did you take time to stretch your brain in many directions by using your creativity to help you take the material and apply it to a bigger picture? Did you develop some hypotheses, come up with a new idea, or invent something?

Barnett goes on to say that we need to stop learning and start thinking *from our own unique perspective*.[23] We all have a passion for a topic that excites us. Barnett says not to spend time studying the field, but rather *be* the field. Become engrossed in your passion so that you live and breathe the subject matter. Newton and Einstein became the subject matter by using their whole being to embrace a field of study. Finally, the moment arrived when all of their thoughts took their place in the puzzle they were attempting to solve and—Eureka!—they discovered a theory to explain a concept.

I think this is why meditation and mindfulness are so important. Unless we clear our minds of the clutter and obsessive thoughts we deal with daily, we will not be able to think. If we are not able to think, we cannot express ourselves to the world. We become a product of a society that may not share our values, takes us away from our purpose, and causes us stress. Meditation and mindfulness will help us think, through the use of relaxation, self-awareness, and being present in the moment. We will be able to be ourselves.

Your parents deserve the opportunity to be themselves as they age and share their unique talents and gifts with the world. If you and your parents are not meditating already, the best way to start is with the examples above or guided meditation. There are websites with free guided meditations, which are in the endnotes for this chapter.[24] [25] There are also classes to join if you find that you cannot consistently find a quiet setting to practice meditation or feel the need for the support of a community as you incorporate this into your everyday life.

SLEEP

Sleep is essential for our bodies to rest and recover from each day's activities. It's common, due to our busy lifestyles, to sacrifice sleep to achieve all of the daily tasks we need to accomplish. However, in the long run, not getting a good night's sleep puts us at risk for disease, illness, and depression.

Our bodies depend on sleep for all of our systems—cognitive function, molecular stability, energy balance, alertness, and mood. Hormones are released as you sleep to help repair cells and regulate the body's use of energy. People who are lacking sleep tend to be less productive, and have difficulty paying attention, reasoning, and problem-solving. They may also be prone to depression and moodiness—leading to less effective interactions with others—and are at a higher risk of getting into traffic accidents.[26]

Sleep acts as a way to clean our brain of all of the debris that accumulates from the information we take in during the day that we do not need to remember.[27] Sleep also reinforces the things we learned during the day that we need to remember. Sleep is essential for both stabilizing previously acquired motor memories and maintaining the brain's efficacy to undergo plastic changes to learn new skills.[28] Think of a time that after a good night's sleep, you could remember the details you needed to know, but which were so hard to grasp when you were exhausted the day before. Memory is dependent on sleep. [29]

In addition to getting a good night's sleep, your parents will also benefit from taking a break during the day. Resting, sometimes called downtime, replenishes the brain's stores of attention and motivation. It is a time when you can let your mind wander and think about past experiences that have influenced you as well as plan for the future. A refreshed feeling after having some respite encourages productivity, performance, and your sense of self.[30]

On average, adults need seven to eight hours of quality sleep per night. Stimulants such as caffeine and certain medications can disrupt sleep. New parents find out very quickly how sleep deprivation feels.

The light from electronic devices such as cell phones, TVs, tablets, and e-readers can prevent you from falling asleep. Insomnia and sleep apnea are the two most common sleep disorders. There are treatments for sleep disorders, which may be as simple as changing your routine or adding herbal tea to your evening routine.

Good sleep is critical for you and your parents' health. To make each day a safe and productive one, make sure you get a good night's sleep.

The benefits of sleep include the following:

- Keeps your heart healthy
- May prevent cancer
- Reduces stress
- Reduces inflammation
- Makes you more alert
- Improves your memory
- May help you lose weight
- May reduce your risk of depression
- Helps the body and brain repair themselves

Suggestions for preparing for a good night's sleep include the following:

- Shut off electronics at least one hour before going to sleep
- Limit napping to 30 minutes a day
- Have a comfortable pre-bedtime routine
- Meditate before going to sleep
- Go to bed early and have a regular bedtime
- Have a comfortable mattress and pillow
- Do not read or eat in bed
- Avoid certain foods in the evening including citrus, spicy, heavy, fatty and fried foods
- Exercise during the day

It is our job to actively take control of our body's primary functions and learn how to breathe, eat, drink, meditate, and sleep well. There will be an opportunity to use the information you learned in this chapter in your therapeutic encounters with your parents through education and use of the health tools.

12

REAL LIFE JUST SHOWED UP

*For after all, the best thing one can do
when it is raining, is to let it rain.*

—Henry Wadsworth Longfellow

D o you remember a time of enjoying a blissful state because your life was running so smoothly? Possibly the credit cards were paid off, there wasn't one appliance in your home that needed to be repaired or replaced, and a letter arrived in the mail awarding your child a scholarship to a performing arts college. Peace and security enveloped your life and allowed the pleasure of a heart full of gratitude. Then came the crushing news: the foundation of your house is caving in. A feeling of doom hits, and now it is time to respond. Life has its share of disappointments. The events you can't control are ones you have to manage.

Each one of us has a set of values and expectations for our life, based on our background of knowledge, experiences, and creative thoughts. When our expectations are not met, we have to *face the music*, as they say, and deal with it. If your life has been smooth sailing up to this point, it may be hard to imagine that daily challenges are a part of normal life. We may feel as though we have our life under control, but this feeling can change rapidly.

Prepare yourself for the unexpected events you will confront. I believe you can do this by being kind to yourself, planning for your future, living each moment with gusto, and leaving regret behind. Learn to manage the rough seas you encounter during this time of life to stay strong, healthy, and focused. Let's visit a few real-life scenarios that may be a part of your future.

DISAPPOINTMENTS

You have just started caregiving for your mother, and you are excited to start the process of therapeutic encounters. The two of you enjoy outings in the community. You notice an article in the newspaper advertising an art exhibit that would be of interest to your mother, a former art teacher, and art enthusiast. A plan to visit the art museum is orchestrated, which includes a concert over lunch. You took the day off of work and spent a significant amount of time planning this exceptional experience. The two of you have talked about how you would like this activity to include sensory stimulation through hearing the music, seeing the art, challenging standing balance, and smelling and tasting favorite foods. You both are also looking forward to the exercise opportunities involving movements during transferring in and out of a car, walking up and down stairs, and strolling through the galleries.

The morning of the outing, you call your mother to remind her that you will pick her up in an hour. She states that she has been experiencing flu symptoms this morning and can't go on the outing. You let her know that you are leaving your home now so you can spend the day to help her recover. As you hang up the phone, you feel worried and your heart sinks as you were looking forward to an inspiring experience for your mother and yourself. These are feelings of disappointment that come from an unexpected event paired with the desire and devotion to help your loved one.

Additional potential scenarios that may have you feeling discouraged could include a lack of motivation from your parents to participate in therapeutic encounters, limited resources available for opportunities, and a decline in their physical health.

If loved ones do not want to participate in your plans for therapeutic encounters, it may take some creativity to convince them to welcome your assistance. Use the information in this book to educate your parents on the benefits of healthy living. Then have a conversation about their thoughts and feelings. Determine if they perceive a roadblock to participating in exceptional experiences. Help them to understand that this is a lifelong process and they can start at their beginning and proceed as they are able. This may be a time of transition and they may feel stuck and unable to move forward. Be patient with them and continue to educate on healthy lifestyle techniques.

You can also use motivational strategies along with helping your parents transition during the changes they are going through. This may help them accept your invitation. If these solutions are not working, seek the assistance of a professional with your parents' permission. A doctor can evaluate the circumstances to determine if there are any barriers to activities and exercise that are related to health issues. This will help you know if you need to adjust your plans for therapeutic encounters or if you need to respect your loved ones' decisions and change your goals.

If you have done everything you can to educate and motivate them and they still decline your help, you have to accept it. There is a saying: *Love them where they are.* Although this is what we need to do, it goes against our human nature to let go of our goals to help others. You may view this as a conflict between you and your parents—what you want for your parents and what they want. The disappointment you feel is due to your desire to provide what you believe is best for your parents. Keep that thought in mind as you manage your feelings.

FAMILY RELATIONSHIPS

You may have thought sibling rivalry was intense when you were young. That was until mom and dad needed help—and it came back with a vengeance. Do you recall the chapter when we talked about sailing and stormy seas? Well, this is an example of one of those turbulent times.

Conflict does not happen within all families. Many can find ways to live harmoniously with each other despite the difference in each one's perspective of what is best for mom and dad. Unfortunately, the tension that arises from conflict can break some families apart. Prevent this by taking steps to ensure you respect everyone's opinion, acknowledge your parents' needs, and pay attention to your own needs.

Conflict arises around different viewpoints on how to provide care. Many people in your parents' lives tell you what is best for them. There may be emotional issues tied to each person's opinion. This could lead to many complicated days and trying times ahead. Conflict resolution will most certainly be a part of your future as you settle disputes and come to terms with decisions. This process is essential so that you can move forward, maintain relationships, and take care of your parents.

CONFLICT RESOLUTION

There are several steps you can take to avoid and resolve conflicts so they don't get the best of you and your family as you care for your parents:

1. Have family meetings to talk about what your parents want and how each sibling can contribute with their specialized skills and resources. Keep the meetings focused on the issues. Use an agenda with objectives and goals, if needed, to keep everyone organized and on task. Take time to express opinions, but remember to focus on the problems to be solved, not on family drama. Stay calm and use a supportive tone of voice, even during disagreements. This goes a long way in keeping peace and working toward a successful solution.

2. Take time to share emotions and feelings in a non-threatening way. Take a break from caregiving and go out with your siblings to enjoy dinner or a favorite event. Make it a priority to take time to relax and have fun. Concentrate on the positive aspects of living that bring you joy and happiness. Reminisce about happy childhood memories or highlights of your parents' lives—or take a break from talking about it. This brings you together and displays what you have in common. Focusing on similarities helps to balance out the times when you feel tension with each other due to conflict of opinions.

3. Stay in the present to keep moving forward. Do not dwell on what you wish was happening rather than what the facts are. Seek professional advice to learn about and understand all of the options in healthcare, housing, and various services.

4. Identify underlying stressors such as siblings who refuse to participate in caregiving, dwindling resources, and emotional issues that may arise. Analyze the feelings causing stress. Name how you feel, such as underappreciated, angry, fearful, or grieving. Understanding what you are feeling helps you to address the stressor. Reach out for help if you need support to manage these issues.

5. Stay focused on your strengths and know that you cannot change others. Accept what is happening in context to this period of life by staying in the present moment. Forgive others so that you can be free of the burden of feeling angry. The anger can affect you emotionally, and decrease your quality of life and the care you are providing. It is essential to *let it go* and enjoy the present moment.

6. Many families avoid important issues and focus on insignificant details, which takes them away from the sole purpose of meeting their parents' needs. If you find that your family is getting stuck and cannot agree on major decisions due to denial and emotional issues, it's time to seek the assistance of a mediator as an objective third party. They can see through the trivial matters and help solve the real problems so you can move forward.

Don't hesitate to look for resources to help you identify weaknesses and build the skills you need to succeed as a caregiver. It is much easier to avoid problems or to take care of them as they arise than wait until they become difficult to manage. This helps you and your family members maintain clear minds and keep the lives of loved ones as the primary focus.

CAREGIVER BURNOUT

We all think we are immune from getting burned out until we find ourselves exhausted, ill, depressed, hopeless, anxious, and not interested in our life anymore. These are some of the classic symptoms of caregiver burnout. Other symptoms include a change in appetite and sleep patterns, irritability, and excessive use of alcohol and medications. You may even get so burned out you want to hurt yourself or the person you are helping. Take these signs seriously. You need to step into action immediately and work on recovering your health. This may mean decreasing your commitment or giving up the role of primary caregiver. No one's life is perfect; however, your life can be balanced.

Ways to avoid burnout include the following:

1. Take care of yourself. Make sure you take enough time every day for sleep, exercise, meditation, nutrition, and socialization. You need a village, too!
2. Ask for help from family, friends, volunteer groups, and support groups. Delegate tasks and errands to be done such as housekeeping, grocery shopping, and laundry. Find out about the family-leave benefits at work to allow more hours in the day to provide caregiving.
3. Practice gratitude. You will be amazed at how this changes your life. In fact, this is an example of building positive neural networks. It works!
4. Take a break and get away. Leave town for the weekend or an extended vacation. Find resources such as respite care, a caregiving team, and the support of others to take care of loved ones. Permit yourself to step away from the caregiving role, take a well-deserved break, and do not take guilt with you on your trip.
5. Join support groups to strengthen yourself emotionally and build up resilience. You have the right to say "no"

to placing too much burden on yourself. Ask for the support of others to lead the way for you.

6. Find support through education online, in books, and seminars on the aging process and caregiving. The knowledge of various disease processes, resources in your area, and caregiving gives you peace of mind and confidence when you need to make decisions about your parents' healthcare and housing options.

As you and your family take care of your parents, you will most likely find out that you each bring something different to the table of caregiving. Every one of you has a personal relationship with your parents. Although you and your siblings may have grown up within a few years of each other, you find out that you each see the past, as well as the present stage of life, through your own unique set of eyes. You won't agree on every aspect of caregiving, but you can agree that you have similarities and differences when it comes to what you think is suitable for your parents. Using your own set of skills and abilities to provide for their needs enhances your parents' lives.

Your emotions may be vulnerable at first as you take on this role, and you feel the loss for your parents as well as yourself. As time goes on, you can learn to put life and loss into perspective and turn your focus to cherishing the time you have with your parents.

You will find that your parents each have particular needs, strengths, weaknesses, likes, and dislikes. There are physical, mental, and emotional factors that affect each person throughout their entire life. This is demonstrated in the way they perceive, process, and respond to situations. Your parents use the skills they have learned throughout their lifetime to deal with the changes that are happening to their bodies and minds. Some people will be confident and resilient while others are afraid and cower when faced with adversity. Whatever their response is, it is essential to respect their individuality.

Most of us try to do our best in life, although at times, we fail. We have a deep desire to be loved and honored—and so do our parents. Refrain from judging them. Take time for hugs and saying, "I love you"—even if you don't find those sentiments reciprocated. If you are finding this process makes you uneasy, find a middle ground where you feel content. If mental health issues arise, they are best dealt with by professional guidance.

When real life shows up, there will be periods of choppy water to navigate. There could be disagreements about the quality or direction of healthcare for your parents, safety issues putting your parents at risk, or old family struggles can resurface. Many find that caring for parents when there are multiple family members involved brings tension and stress leading to divisions in the family, which are not necessary. At this time, it is wise to use conflict resolution and have the influence and guidance of a third party or trained professional to give the family direction.

It is always a positive move to place importance on your relationship with your family. It may take a conscious decision to do this, but in the long-run, you will see the benefits of keeping your family ties strong. If you have tried every way to reach out with love, care, and compassion to your family and it does not work, then you may have to take a different approach—sometimes you have to love people from a distance.

Years after your parents are gone, you may look back and wonder why you chose to fight a particular battle, which was not significant as time went on. At times it can be difficult to remain rational when your emotions are in a heightened state. This is a time for self-assessment, and it may help to reach out to others for their opinion on a topic that is upsetting you. Moving forward is your goal. Use the health tools and methods in this book to take a proactive approach to aging and improve the lives of yourself and those you love.

13

CAUTION: CHANGE AHEAD

Vulnerability is the birthplace of innovation,
creativity and change.

—Brené Brown

Now it is time to address how to deal with the gains and the losses in life during the aging years. Let's face it: aging is a mixed bag. The beautiful parts of aging may include an increase in wisdom, insight, knowledge, and patience. Viewing the world through mature eyes is a benefit of the years spent gaining wrinkles and gray hair. Problems that occur with aging include failing eyesight and hearing, memory loss, and the aches and pains that appear when joints are wearing out. There are many factors, such as lifestyle and genetics, that affect the rate at which we age. Aging is not an event. It's a process.

There are many joys during these years for your parents, which may include seeing grandchildren fall in love and get married, the birth of great-grandchildren, and developing new aspects of themselves. There are also the heartaches endured as beloved spouses and friends depart this world, and they face the losses associated with aging. The most common transitions in these years include retirement, relocation, and bereavement. Support of family and friends is needed as our parents grieve the emptiness of losses, celebrate the beauty and opportunities of the present time, and look forward to the future.

Transitions have been a part of our journey through life as we developed from children into adults. Growth is appreciated at all levels of our existence as we mature and develop new skills, take on more responsibility, and accept more complex roles. The overall result of transition is stability in our lives. Transitions are not temporary, shallow changes. They entail tangible outward behaviors and personal beliefs that mark a fundamental shift in our view of ourselves and the world.[1] To continue to progress through life, we must make transitions. It is a process of letting go, learning, doing, and accepting that you can help your parents with by using the information below.

In his book, *Transitions: Making Sense of Life's Changes*, William Bridges describes stages to depict how people evolve during the transition experience.[2] The first stage of transition, according to Bridges, is a *period of endings*. It is caused by an event that brings about an upheaval or dramatic change in the balance of our lives, such as an accident or illness. It could also occur when we have increased self-awareness or see a situation in a different light. We may feel stuck or paralyzed. At this time, it is evident that the old ways in which we functioned no longer suit us, and we see the need for transformation in our lives. It is a time to let go of the past, reinvent the future, and rediscover a sense of self. Emotions that may arise include denial, shock, anger, frustration, and anxiety which are reactions to the process.[3]

The second stage is the *neutral zone*. This is the in-between time when a person is in an ambiguous state. They have not parted with the old ways so they cannot be fully functional in the new expression of identity and behaviors. During this time, your parents are in a state of not moving forward or backward. Time spent in this phase brings about a chance to be open to new possibilities. You can offer support by giving your loved ones time to process the opportunities ahead of them and grieve the past they are releasing. They may feel bombarded with helpful suggestions of what they should be doing. They will need time alone to think about what they want in their next phase of life.

Assistance with knowledge related to the changes they experience is helpful as they go through this period. For example, if your parents have to move to an assisted living facility from their home, a visit to the facility or a brochure highlighting the positive aspects of the new living situation may provide comfort and confidence in the future. Use multiple sources of information to help your parents understand and process this transition. This phase may occur during an illness that requires a period of rehabilitation where new skills for mobility develop and adapted living is accepted. Although your parents may be uncertain and skeptical about this new stage in life, the education and experiences gained during time spent in the neutral zone help them start to embrace the idea of change.

The final stage is *new beginnings*. Your parents are now finding meaning and purpose in life while experiencing some control in their new roles. They may display impatience as well as hope and enthusiasm. The three stages need to be traveled through and completed for a successful transition, although not necessarily in order. Understanding the transition process helps you identify what stage your parents are in. This last stage is the time when your parents are finally able to be comfortable with the changes and embrace the new skills needed to be successful in their current status. The transition period is over, and they can enjoy stability again. Transitions encompass the entire time from the beginning of the event until your parents have grown and accepted their new situations.

At the time of your parents' transitions, be present to explain the circumstances of what is happening, give clear reasons for the need for change, and listen while encouraging them to express their emotions. They have to spend time processing what is happening to them and decide what to leave behind and what to take with them into the next phase. Making changes requires new patterns of response, developing new skills and relationships, and adopting new coping strategies. It is a process occurring over time as your parents travel through the three stages.

Now that you are familiar with the stages of transition, you can periodically assess your parents' progress. Determine which stage they are in and track their progress, or decline, as they are in the process. Look for positive signs during a transition such as a high level of physical and mental functioning, a sense of being connected to their friends and family, actions of empowerment as they take control of their lives, and feelings of integrity or wholeness. In healthy transitions, you see a progression toward being full of life. In unhealthy transitions, you see a trend toward the risk of weakness and illness.

Some people are not able to make transitions for various reasons. They may go through a change, such as being dependent on caregivers and never truly find acceptance and identity in the new situation. Part of *your* transition is the acceptance that they are not able to make the transition due to beliefs, a cognitive state, or physical abilities.

Although everyone strives for successful transitions, there is a normal flux between healthy and unhealthy transitions. Your parents will sense the pull between moving forward and embracing the change and the past tugging them back into their familiar patterns. Here are some recommendations on how to enhance the healthy aspects of transitions.

REDEFINING MEANINGS

For a healthy transition to occur, you need to redefine meanings.[4] This is a process that takes time as you and your parents discover the meaning of the transition and find new meanings. For example, your parents may need you to explain what is happening during a transition. They may not understand the effects of an illness or that recovery from a traumatic fall with a hip fracture involves time in a rehabilitation facility. Give clear and specific reasons for the change they are experiencing. If they have to move out of their home due to inability to be independent as they did before an illness, give them concrete examples of what they are *not* able to do to take care of themselves. Identify factors to assist them with the transition, such as needing extra assistance through home health care or rehabilitation in a nursing home or hospital. This will help to redefine meanings that relate to their new situation. In unhealthy transitions, there is resistance to redefining meanings.[5] Attempting to apply old definitions to a new situation doesn't help your parents during transitions.

MANAGING MULTIPLE TRANSITIONS

Transitions may happen one at a time, or there may be many to deal with simultaneously. An example of multiple transitions for your loved one would be moving to a nursing home following a hip fracture after suffering the loss of a spouse two months before this event. There are several issues to confront in this situation—grief caused by loss of a spouse and home, pain from a fracture, rehabilitation demands, as well as a new way of life in community living. These can be stressful times for the entire family. Working through all of the transitions may take a team of professionals and a variety of strategies. In addition to family and friends, gerontological nurses, as well as doctors and psychologists, are equipped to assist the person and family with needed resources and medical care.

STRESS AND ANXIETY MANAGEMENT

Anxiety develops as fear of the unknown is encountered. There are periods when your parents face new situations. They may be unsure of the expectations placed on them as well as what outcomes to expect. The future looks different than the past they are leaving behind. They need education from you as well as health professionals and family members or friends who have had similar experiences. Ease their burdens by helping them manage daily living activities. If they are struggling to get dressed or put a meal on the table, their stress level increases. They look for security as well as some control over their lives in times of change. Give them the assistance they need while helping them remain as independent as possible with control over the areas they can manage. Anxiety due to life-changing events can cause increased sickness, loss of initiative, depression, and decreased performance.

Several factors can add stress to your parents' lives, including social losses, environmental factors, inadequate care, social isolation, financial burdens, and chronic illness. Bring awareness of the increased stress to the attention of your loved one if they aren't coping well with the changes. To combat this stress, you can help your parents use existing or develop new coping skills, add social support systems, and address poor care issues.

Start therapeutic encounters that include exercise, diaphragmatic breathing, and meditation to help decrease anxiety and depression. It's also essential to help them express themselves through their unique talents. This helps balance their bodies, minds, and spirits, and aids them in flourishing in their new stations in life.

Advise your parents' doctor if the anxiety and depression are negatively affecting their daily mobility and functions. The attention given to this problem is well worth the benefits. I have seen the results of lifting the burden of anxiety and depression from people. Easing distress allows people the freedom to be able to work toward achieving their goals and moving forward in life. The health tools mentioned in this book, including proper nutrition and hydration, sleep, breath work, exercise, and meditation, are critical at this time and can easily be ignored if a person is experiencing stress and feels anxious. Help your parents realize that this is a solution to the problem and assist them to make time in their day to get these activities accomplished.

CREATIVE ARTS FOR HEALTH PROMOTION

The benefits of using art and creative expression have been found to promote psychological and physiological healing. In her article, *Aging: What's Art Got To Do With It?*, Barbara Began, Ph.D., ATR-BC, states that therapeutic art experiences can supply meaning and purpose in the lives of older adults. The opportunity for expression through art and activities based on meaning, purpose, and honesty brings about feelings of integrity and wisdom rather than feelings of longing and despair.[6]

Gene Cohen, MD, Ph.D., director of the Center on Aging, Health, and Humanities at George Washington University, conducted a study on the impact of art programs on the quality of life.[7] He found that older persons who participated in community-based art programs run by professional artists were found to have benefitted from the effects of health promotion and disease prevention. This led to a positive outcome on maintaining independence and reducing dependency. This appears to ultimately reduce risk factors that support the need for long-term care.

Art can also help build the brain's cognitive reserve as it forms and strengthens neural pathways. Making or viewing art causes the brain to reshape, adapt, and restructure and provides your parents with more efficient and alternative pathways for thinking and problem-solving.[8]

The assisted living facility my mother resides in provides a painting class every other week. I have had a chance to participate several times as family members are welcome to join the class. The painting instructor is exceptionally passionate about her role of engaging the residents and teaching them to paint. She offers group and individual instruction as she demonstrates mixing colors and advanced painting techniques.

The painting class promotes brain function, fine motor skills, and provides social time for building friendships. It also allows the residents to take pride in their work. The group members display their works of art in a biannual art show at the facility. They receive a sense of satisfaction from an accomplishment which builds their self-esteem and positively affects many other areas of their life.

It has been fun to be part of the group and take an interest in the residents and their artwork. The painting class brought us together as a unified group, which aided the transition process for many. It was also a time for relaxation and reducing stress.

The painting instructor told me that she has seen many people use the fine arts after losing a spouse, as a source of comfort and strength as they processed their grief. There are findings that creative engagement in activities such as crafts or artwork helps older people have resilience when faced with mounting challenges during their aging years along with providing cognitive benefits.[9]

Do your parents have a hobby that includes creative expression? The health benefits and promotion of successful aging are reasons to keep them engaged in their favorite art form or help them explore ways to get one started.

LEND AN EAR

Listening to your aging parents is critical. A good listener hears what is said and also picks up on non-verbal cues. The information received is then used to understand circumstances and feelings and to solve problems. Listening also allows your parents to talk through their dilemmas and come up with solutions on their own that make them comfortable. They may have one small issue to work through or a multidimensional situation dealing with a vast array of problems. They need you to help them by listening. Excellent communication starts with listening with an open mind.

I recently watched a movie portraying a family that did not know how to communicate well. In most scenes, there were two to five family members present. They either talked to each other at the same time or replied to each other immediately during a conversation. They did not allow time to listen and process the meaning of the words and the nonverbal cues. There was no thought going into the conversation; therefore, they were not able to functionally respond to each other. At times there were ten ideas thrown out all at once, which ended up in a cloud of smoke with no positive outcomes. This was indeed a one-sided conversation, which led to a series of chaotic scenes. The family was always frustrated but had no insight as to why they felt angry and confused.

The movie was funny at times as the lack of communication skills led to humorous situations. However, I found it to be sad as the family lacked the skills to be functional caregivers and unfortunately missed out on the joy of a fulfilling relationship with their aging father.

I was exhausted from watching the movie. Can you imagine being there in real life? Do your communication skills start with listening? This is an excellent time to assess the strengths and weaknesses of your communication skills to help you manage family dynamics as you travel this road with your parents.

ASSIST WITH NEW TASKS

Many people value their independent lifestyle. They have no intention of making changes and when faced with a transition, they make it known that they want to function at their previous level. There are usually underlying issues for why they are not willing to change. It may take a few conversations to uncover why a change is unacceptable to them. Many times it could be due to anxiety from not knowing what the future holds. Offer assistance to help them learn new skills, provide all of the adaptive equipment needed for mobility and safety, and be patient as they make changes and move toward acceptance.

A study on the transition to needing help with medications found that some older adults became frustrated, depressed, or angry about requiring assistance.[10] The study found that the transition from hospital to home was portrayed by worry. Concerns about learning new skills and distress about disruption in the family's usual activities were among the topics that caused anguish. The participants were able to move from worry to mastery of necessary skills as the transition evolved. Time was a factor in the transition. Two months after discharge from the hospital, new routines were established, and the participants felt in control of their new situations. The data showed a steady decline in anxiety and depression. Transitions take time and patience as we travel from one state of being to another. Assisting your parents to learn new skills can help them experience comfort, confidence, and joy.

MODIFY EXPECTATIONS

Expectations are naturally a part of our life and tend to vary among the generations. Your parents have long-standing expectations that they have placed on themselves and others, which may be difficult to change as they age. As their lives transform during the aging process, modifying expectations is critical for healthy transitions. For example, if your parents have lost the ability to drive a car, being dependent on others for transportation alters their way of life. They may miss the independence that driving to social outings, medical appointments, the grocery store, and place of worship offers them. The fulfillment of an independent lifestyle, social time, and community activities they engage in can change. Modifications are made by planning alternative activities to meet those needs such as finding transportation, having friends and family members make time to visit them in their home, and planning for additional social activities.

Another example is expecting your parents to function at the same physical and mental level. If your parent has a decline in function and cannot ascend a flight of stairs to get to their upstairs bedroom, everyone has to modify their expectations. Providing a bedroom on the first floor will most likely be the only solution if they want to continue to live in their own home. As new circumstances arise, new expectations have to be formed and accepted for a healthy transition.

MAINTAIN CONTINUITY WHILE RESTRUCTURING ROUTINES

Maintaining continuity from your parents' past routines while restructuring daily activities as needed is healthy. Avoiding disruptions that compromise friendships, identity, and the living environment is also important. Attempt to keep as much of their previous life intact to stabilize them while they are coping with changes. At times when daily routines need to be restructured, providing new structures, or finding new methods to help them achieve their daily goals should be done to make the situation manageable, pleasant, and predictable.[11] You can expect that if this is not done, an unhealthy situation will arise, which leads to your parents experiencing a daily life that is haphazard and unorganized. This, in turn, promotes feelings of discontent and emptiness.[12]

Current research is demonstrating that because our brains are plastic, we can build neural networks to accommodate for change. Expecting an aging person to stay in a familiar routine they are comfortable with is acceptable but not necessarily essential. A person can train their brain to accept change by participating in brain training exercises, new (small and large) adventures, and overcoming the fear of failure.[13] Starting at an early age on these brain activities helps us adapt to change and there is less reason to keep daily routines and the environment intact.

While your parent is adjusting to a new routine, help them find opportunities available for activities and hobbies. There may be some hidden treasures such as water aerobics, senior exercise classes, book clubs, art classes, and social outings to enjoy.

You may not realize it, but your brain thrives on pleasant surprises. Take delight in what the world has to offer from near and afar. Be adventurous in your daily activities and keep your mind open to all of the wonderful possibilities waiting to be explored. Your brain will appreciate your efforts.

PERSONAL GROWTH ASSISTANCE

Help your parents discover new avenues to express the personal growth they are experiencing during transitions. Encourage them to spend time with their new friends, pursue a hobby relating to a new level of self-awareness, and gain knowledge or skills related to a needed change. Show your acceptance of their new choices. This enhances their life and solidifies the transition process.

EMOTIONAL SUPPORT

Your parents need to feel secure during this time. Spend extra time with them in person—or by phone or Skype if you can't physically be there. Ask them uncomplicated questions about their experiences and then take the time to listen. They need to express themselves if they are able. Validating their opinions about change is essential. Giving advice is fine if you know they welcome it. You may have to give your opinion in small doses as they adjust to the change. Stating the facts of the transition is good if it is followed up by helpful suggestions to help them move forward. This assists them to let go of the past and embrace the present and the future. Living fully in the moment is the goal.

Emotional issues may surface in this stage. Transitions or a lack of being able to transition could be linked to the past. Letting go of hurts, wrongs, harbored feelings—from others or ourselves—can be a challenge. If releasing a hurtful situation was not handled promptly throughout your parents' lives, they may be hanging onto the pain and experiencing the side effects of bitterness daily. Distress affects their outlook, the way they react to situations, and their relationships. Be aware that this is part of the messy thing we deal with every day called *life*.

Although emotions are normal and needed, they should not be so overwhelming that they negatively affect your parents' life. If your loved one is struggling with issues, you may or may not be able to help them. Treatment for this could be the job of a professional or a spiritual guide. Don't let yourself turn into a counselor if you are not qualified. You need to stay emotionally healthy and avoid feeling like a punching bag.

Healing involves forgiveness of oneself and others. Practicing forgiveness is a gift we give ourselves. It is also a vital part of functioning at our highest level. Love the people in your life as much as you are able, refrain from judging them, and be supportive of their endeavors. Offer as much support as you can as you listen, find activities you both enjoy, and help them obtain the support they need to address their spiritual self.

A Group Therapy Experience—Picasso's Painting Party

Picasso's Painting Party is a group therapy activity I created mainly to work on balance skills. It also works well to spark conversations about talents, personal strengths, and transitions. I like to use Picasso as an example because he was a person who was an artist his entire life. His mother revealed that his first word was "pencil." Art wasn't just a massive part of his life—it *was* his life until his death at age 91. He became obsessed with drawing, which was the only subject he enjoyed in school. He had the same occupation his whole life and found various ways to express himself and his emotion through his art as he transitioned from stage to stage.

I am sure you have seen at least one Picasso painting. What comes to your mind when you hear the name Picasso or see his artwork? I think of *genius*. As I look at his development as an artist, I see his mind and body working together to form what was perfect for his state in life at the time. The art he created, influenced by his spirited personality, is unforgettable. I would have loved to meet him and watch him create. The entertainment alone would be fascinating. It is apparent that he developed as a person and thus found avenues to express himself.

I share the story of Picasso's life with my patients and tell them about how in his early years, 1901 through 1904, Picasso went through the Blue Period, rightly named after his somewhat melancholy and somber blue and grey paintings. Then there were the green and gray paintings he produced of poverty, isolation, and anguish. Picasso was dealing with depression after the loss of a great friend. Recovering from this, he started into the Rose Period from 1905 to 1907, which depicted a lighter, cheery side in a classic style featuring pink rose and light orange tones. The African period appeared in 1908. The colors he used in these paintings were brownish and neutral tones. Following this period, from 1909 to 1912, he co-created Cubism. This style shocked the art world, capturing the essence of the subject on canvas using geometrical shapes, exaggerating certain features. As Picasso continued to develop, he transformed again and went into Classicism and Surrealism genres where he spent the 1920s and 1930s.

As I tell the story of Picasso's life, I want my patients to see how Picasso traveled through many stages, made successful transitions, and used art to express himself as he moved forward. There are many examples of Picasso that demonstrate he was not a passive participant in life. He created over fifty thousand pieces of art over a 75-year career. His work represented periods when he flourished as well as the periods when he struggled. The Cubism style is the result of a life fully lived.

My patients then have time to relate Picasso's journey to the periods of their lives and reflect on how they adapted and changed in response to their circumstances. I prompt my patients to share some of the evolutions they had during challenging periods in their lives. By thinking of the times they made successful conversions, they realize they used their strengths to transition from one period to another. They think about what it took to achieve the growth and the results they found by working toward the goal of transition. The conversation then shifts to talk about the losses they are experiencing due to illness or injury and the work they are doing in rehabilitation to reclaim their lives and reach their fullest potential.

There are three main objectives for this group activity. One is discussing the life and career of Picasso, which involves looking at his artwork in the various periods of his life. This includes bringing up the subject of transitions as his artwork changed with each period of his life. Sample discussion questions are included below. Use your creativity and genius to change the questions to fit the needs of your loved ones.

The second purpose of this group therapy is the activity and exercise aspect. Each patient, if able, is assisted to stand up and walk to the easel to participate in painting a group picture. The first participant starts the picture, and it is added to by each member of the group. Each patient receives at least two opportunities to paint on the canvas. During this movement portion, after they walk up to the canvas, each patient is instructed to stand facing the canvas using a narrow base of support, or feet together, as they paint a portion of the picture. The second time they stand up to paint, they use a wide base of support, or feet apart, as they paint the picture. They are asked to feel the difference in stability and balance between the two different stances. Most feel confident and secure with feet apart and notice feeling off balance when they have their feet together. Later we discuss how this can relate to doing activities at home such as reaching into the cupboard with a wide base of support rather than a narrow base of support for stability and safety.

A goal of the group therapy is to discuss a strength or talent they have that serves them well as they go through rehabilitation. We liken this to Picasso who used his creative, artistic talent through good times and bad. Some residents are interested and engaged—while others aren't. One aspect most people enjoy is painting the picture. We then hang the pictures up in the therapy gym for a few days where they can admire their creativity and hard work. While viewing the artwork, it gives us another chance to reiterate the benefits of using a wide base of support to maintain balance and safety when they go home and are reaching outside of their base of support.

The most memorable time I experienced when using this group therapy session was when we had two separate painting groups in the room. After the general discussion and instructions were complete, one therapist was assisting half of the participants through the painting portion of the activity at one end of the therapy gym, and I was on the other end leading my group to paint. It appeared that all was going well. I noted that her group was painting a lovely scenic picture, and my group was having fun painting the cubism shapes. I looked over to admire the other group's painting and noticed their canvas had beautiful rolling hills, an apple tree, wavy stream, blue sky with a bird sailing through it, and sunshine over a rainbow. I glanced back at my group's painting and saw quite a different scenario. There it was: a nude lady made up of triangles, rectangles, and circles. I could feel my face start to flush and hurried to assist the next patient up to the easel and guided her hand with the paintbrush to place a swimming suit on the lady. I looked back at my group and saw a few smirks on their faces. Never underestimate the creativity of a group!

The questions below can be used in this group therapy session to addresses transitions:

- How has your life has changed in the past few years?
- How did these changes affect your life as you knew it?
- What strengths did you use to help you get through the transitions as you aged?
- Who helped you manage these transitions?
- Where are you in the process of transitioning from your past to your present life?
- How can I and others help you with your transition?

As you are involved in an activity with your parents, praise them and point out their strengths. Make your comments specific and generous. Something like, "Great job, Mom, you just stood for 15 minutes, mixing up a batch of cookies." Or, "Wow, Dad, you just walked to the garden and back to the house over some difficult terrain and kept your balance." Place a loving hand on their shoulder as you give them these comments. This takes a teachable moment and solidifies it, which builds confidence and the desire to continue to achieve goals.

Life hands us joys and sorrows. None of us can escape the challenges we are faced with if we intend to live life fully. The way we proceed through transitions with an open mind, a creative spirit, and finally the acceptance of our new self is our ticket to freedom to enjoy our next step and create our best self. This is information we can pass on to our aging parents with love and grace.

14

MAKE IT HAPPEN

It ain't over till it's over.

—Yogi Berra

I enjoy Yogi-isms from one of the most famous baseball players ever. He was able to put a twist on words that made you reflect and laugh at the same time. I'm sure Yogi Berra set goals to achieve his success and fame. After reading his many quotes, fondly referred to as Yogi-isms, it appears he had a goal to reach people through his witty comments.

His baseball goals may have included using his fantastic talents effectively and consistently. His quote above tells us something about goals. As I see it, you need to set a goal, not lose sight of it, and work with focus and persistence to achieve it.

Imagine a baseball game, the score is close, and it is the bottom of the ninth inning. The losing team is up at bat to win the game. The manager, coaches, and players put forth their best effort, trickiest plays, longest hits, and lightning speed to work toward the goal of winning the game. If they succeed and win, you might use the words "they got lucky" to describe the end of the game.

We all have a day now and then when we receive a surprise in our life, and we feel lucky. Although we wouldn't give those times back, we know we can't count on luck to be there for us—and that's why they call it luck. What we can count on is the success we find when we do the hard work it takes during daily practice, apply discipline and effort, and take the necessary steps to accomplish what we set out to do. As your parents set goals and work toward them, they have a win—and it has nothing to do with luck.

A quote from Mickey Mantle worth reading is, "Somebody once asked me if I ever went up to the plate trying to hit a home run. I said, 'Sure, every time.'" Mantle built his life around baseball as he invested time and energy in his goals. Because of this, he became a household name as a great American baseball player. By setting short-term goals to achieve daily success, he fulfilled his long-term goal of being in the league of the greatest baseball players. He set a goal for every time he stepped up to the plate.

Goals are an essential part of life. One of the best ways to determine if you are working toward what you want in life is to set a goal formally. I believe we all have a purpose in life, which is sometimes called our vision. When we are busy and working toward meeting our everyday responsibilities, we may forget we have a purpose—and lose sight of our vision. However, it never truly leaves us. It is the big picture of how and what we want our life to look like—what we want to satisfy our souls' craving for meaning.

At some point in our lives we may feel we have achieved our purpose. Still, most of us would agree we have not accomplished everything in life we have set out to do. A fulfilled life includes working toward or living in our purpose every day. If the vision and the goals are not in place, we can quickly be taken off course by all kinds of distractions.

Setting goals and working toward them during therapeutic experiences with a loved one helps you both work toward what is important in your lives. It will also keep you organized as you face challenges. Remember the saying—"Keep your eye on the ball." In other words, it takes laser focus to hit this one out of the park. Staying on task and being committed helps everyone. Goals can help you stay focused. There are guidelines in this book to make the process of goal writing simple.

By setting goals, your parents can measure their achievement, which increases their self-confidence. There are two kinds of goals: short-term and long-term. Short-term goals can be achieved within a few weeks or months, and long-term goals could take months or years. After you have written down your goals, you must apply an activity or action to the goal. The therapeutic encounters are opportunities to accomplish some or most of the activities. As you have had a chance to absorb the knowledge of this book, you know that the experiences revolve around activities that are well suited for the individual. I advise you to write out your goals and your parents' goals. You can follow the instructions below.

As you are making plans to set goals, consider following the method George T Doran developed using the pneumonic acronym SMART to describe the five attributes of solid goals.[14]

- Specific—Focus on a detailed area for improvement
- Measurable—Determine how you will measure progress
- Achievable—Decide on a highly desirable objective
- Realistic—Choose a goal that is possible with the time and resources you have
- Time-Bound—Set a date when the goal can be achieved

Here are some topics and questions for you and your parents to talk about to lead to goal setting:

- What is important to you in your life right now?

- What are one strength and one weakness you possess? How would you change the weakness?
- What would you like to do today if you had no limits?
- Whom would you like to visit if you had the chance?
- What would you like to accomplish if you had the time and energy?
- What project did you start that you would like to finish?
- If you could do something better, what would that be?

After you have visited with your parents using the questions above, start talking about their goals, desires, and future. You may find out that they want to visit an old childhood friend or a family member before their mobility declines to the point where it is impossible to travel. They may have a spiritual strength or weakness they would like to spend time on in meditation, worship, or community service. An unfinished project they would like to complete would also make a perfect goal.

If your parent wants to do something that seems unattainable, use your creativity to help them get as close as they can to their desired goal. If it is impossible to travel to see the childhood friend, arrange a phone call, Skype, or FaceTime visit for the two of them. If your parent would like to go fishing, you may have to work on standing balance and stair climbing to be able to get in a boat or walk up and down stairs to get to the dock. Not every dream and desire your parents have is obtainable, but you can still honor and validate your loved ones' desires for the future. Place a goal that may not seem reasonable in the long-term category. It is something your parents can look forward to in the future. We all need hope to keep us engaged in life. It also helps the time pass as we strive for a goal.

As you talk about goals and the activities you will be doing to achieve the goals, discuss the support system in place to assist with the goals. Find out who your parents want to have involved in their lives as they work toward their goals. Offer suggestions of organizations and people willing to assist with activities, exercise, and friendship. Talk about the roles they play in the life of your parent. Identify any adverse situations or people in your loved ones' lives who are not supportive of their future goals.

Use the goal worksheet at the end of this chapter to fill out short-term and long-term goals. If your parent is not able to participate in goal setting, write some reasonable goals for them or yourself as a caregiver. Include other family members, friends, and caregivers in the goal writing if it is appropriate and helpful. They may be able to assist with the therapeutic encounters and could have some input on activities. If the goals you've written aren't achievable, and it is evident, you can revise them as necessary.

If your parents are active participants in writing goals, you can use the following questions to help them recognize their unique strengths and abilities. Help them feel empowered to take on an active role in the experiences.

- What roles did you take on at home or in the workplace?
- How did these roles help you achieve your goals in the family and work environments?
- Who assisted you during those times?
- Who can help assist you now with your goals?
- How did you help other family members or friends achieve their goals?

To achieve the goals, your parents need to be active participants. Make the activities fun, enjoyable, and suited to their intelligences. The goals may range from getting out of bed by 8:30 in the morning to working out in the gym three times a week. Whatever it is, make it a relevant part of their life and let them know that their participation is vital.

Below is an example showing how to set goals:

Long-term goal: Start a new hobby   Date: June 18
of fishing on the lake.

Short term goal: Buy or rent a boat.   Date: June 1
Activities:
    a. Research locations to shop for or rent a boat.
    b. Go shopping for the boat.
    c. Purchase a boat and trailer or plan to rent the boat.

Short term goal: Purchase fishing equipment.   Date: May 15
Activities:
    a. Take inventory of existing equipment.
    b. Shop for fishing equipment.
    c. Pack equipment for a fishing trip.

Short term goal: Secure a fishing license.   Date: May 30
Activities:
    a. Call the local licensure department.
    b. Make plans to purchase a fishing license.
    c. Purchase a fishing license.

Short term goal: Improve standing   Date: June 1
balance to step in the boat.
Activities:
    a. Work on strengthening exercises three times a week.
    b. Work on balance exercises five times a week.
    c. Practice walking on uneven surfaces and stairs three
       times a week with assistance.

Here is a worksheet for you to use:

Long-term goal: _____Date: _____

Short-term goal:_____Date: _____
Activities:
    a.
    b.
    c.

Short-term goal:_____Date: _____
Activities:
    a.
    b.
    c.

Short-term goal:_____Date: _____
Activities:
    a.
    b.
    c.

Recording your parents' achievements during their participation in the activities by taking pictures or keeping a journal is an excellent way to celebrate their accomplishments. The pictures can be placed on a poster or in a picture album to be displayed for others to see. You can imagine the pride they feel as they graduate from one step to another and finally reach their goal. The pictures, along with the stated goals, is a treasure they can share. Caring individuals involved in your parents' lives are happy to partake in the joy that surrounds the accomplishments. Praise and attention are motivating and will help your parents stay interested in working toward their future goals.

As baseball great Ted Williams once said, "A man has to have goals—for a day, for a lifetime—and that was mine: to have people say, 'There goes Ted Williams, the greatest hitter who ever lived.'" Creating goals with your parents allow each person to have a purpose and plan for the days ahead.

PART THREE:

THE FOUR-STEP METHOD

15

HERE WE GO!

No man ever steps in the same river twice,
for it's not the same river and he's not the same man.

—Heraclitus

Now we have finally reached the time to start Experi-Age, the four-step method. This chapter explains the process of building a therapeutic encounter with the tools you have learned in Part Two of this book. The next four chapters each contain one step of the method which includes building and implementing the experiences.

The goal of building a therapeutic encounter is to provide an exceptional experience that affects the body, mind, and soul. There is a structured outline for you to work from in each chapter that directs you through sequencing the process and setting up the therapeutic encounter. Each step includes an introduction, activity or experience, reflection, processing, generalizing, and application. You do not have to use all of the questions in each category. Use the questions that pertain to your parents during each encounter. I recommend using a journal, notebook, or electronic page to write out your plan. Record the answers to the questions you and your parents discuss as you may want to refer to them at a later time when you reflect and plan.

THE FOUR-STEP METHOD

Step 1: Who I Am
Step 2: Life Vision and Goal Setting
Step 3: Empowerment Through Concrete Activities
Step 4: Assessing Therapeutic Encounters and Goals

These steps, or stages, are dynamic. They are not meant to be rigid formulas. Do not get stuck in a step. If you are not making progress, move on or go back to a step that needs more attention. For example, if your parents cannot focus on finding their strengths during Step 1, move on to Step 2. They may not be able to identify their strengths if they are in the process of making a difficult transition. There is no need to waste time. Proceed to the next step they are capable of participating in and go back to Step 1 when they are ready.

If your parents are confident and goal oriented, they can spend very little time in the first two steps and start working on the activities that help them accomplish their goals. Starting over or moving to the middle or end-stage to capture what you need at that moment is acceptable. The goal is to make gains in each area at the pace that works for you and your parents.

As you move from step to step and see your parents progressing in an upward fashion with increasing cognitive function and functional mobility, set higher goals. Due to illness, dementia, or natural decline you may find that they are not going to achieve a particular goal. At this time, downgrade or change the goal to fit your parents' needs. If you are questioning why they are declining, address these issues with professionals who can guide you with the knowledge of disease processes, test for illnesses, and give you expected and appropriate functional levels to base your future goals on.

At the time goal achievement occurs, your parents can continue doing the activities from the therapeutic encounters in an informal way, such as with exercise classes, as a way to maintain their progress. Then they can spend time on self-assessment to determine what new goals they would like to set. This dynamic process does not end. As development occurs in body, mind, and soul, a positive journey through the aging years takes place. Enjoy this time and help your parents celebrate their accomplishments.

As time goes on, it is natural that their life's vision and goals will change as they approach the end of their life. Be prepared to help them focus on what is important to them when this stage arrives.

You may have already started the therapeutic encounters. Many people who have a vibrant family culture, are open to communication, and enjoy spending time participating in activities together are already aboard the ship. Some families may find resistance to getting started. This would be an excellent time to spend developing relationships by listening to each other and finding commonalities to share and develop further.

Each person is unique, so keep an open mind and stay relaxed about the process. Refrain from severe intensity while planning these experiences. Creative flow can be achieved if you relax, breathe deeply, and open your mind to possibilities.

To motivate your parents, highlight the progress they make, even if it is a tiny step forward. Give them immediate feedback on what they did right. If a decline takes place, focus on the positive aspects of their mobility and function.

In early life, as well as when we move into our aging years, we are motivated more by social incentives than warning signs. For example, it is not helpful to tell your parents that if they do not participate in exercises and stay healthy, they will live in misery. Those words are *not* motivating. Fear makes people anxious and causes them to freeze up and not take action.

What will more than likely set them into motion is a little healthy competition. A friend once told me her mother, Anne, wouldn't do anything at home to help herself with mobility or a healthy lifestyle, despite being very productive and able in her younger years. Anne had settled into a life of sitting all day in front of the television and was starting to become weak and dependent on others. After a few years of this lifestyle, she developed an illness and had to be hospitalized. Anne was not strong enough to return home, so she was transferred to a nursing home for rehabilitation. My friend was pleased that her mother's dormant competitive spirit found new life.

She told me that one day when Anne was sitting in the therapy gym waiting to work on walking skills, she struck up a conversation with a man sitting next to her who had just finished his walk. She was curious to know how far he was able to walk, and he told her he had walked one hundred feet. Although she was not able to walk more than sixty feet up to that point, she decided if he could walk one hundred feet, she could walk one hundred and twenty feet—and she did! Giving your parents examples of their peers achieving milestones and goals by participating in healthy lifestyle choices can be helpful.

Don't wait to start this process until you think you have it perfected. If you feel overwhelmed, think of this exercise as taking a small piece of the puzzle, putting it where it belongs, and moving on to the next piece. Keep placing the pieces where they fit without knowing what the final picture will look like. In the end, you have a framework for the vision, a method with a step-by-step procedure, and, finally, a picture that is put together and makes sense.

None of us know what our picture will look like until we finish. The beauty of this process lies in the creativity of the individual. Remember, we are creating ourselves. There are some trials and errors to work through. It's better to get started now than wait for the future. Your actions don't have to be perfect, but they do have to begin to get your adventure in motion.

To get started, open your journal and spend some time finding out about yourself and your parents. Answer these questions prior to planning the therapeutic encounters:

1. Name the three strongest intelligences you have:
   a. _____ b._____ c. _____

   Name the three strongest intelligences your parents have:
   a. _____ b. _____ c. _____
   a. _____ b. _____ c. _____

2. Name two ways to stimulate the senses that your parents would enjoy:
   a. Sight: _____
   b. Touch: _____
   c. Smell: _____
   d. Taste: _____
   e. Sound: _____
   f. Proprioception: _____

3. Name three activities or hobbies your parents have always enjoyed:
   a. _____
   b. _____
   c. _____

4. Name one way to add breathing to *your* day. Then do the same for meditation.
   a. _____
   b. _____

5. Describe two ways to add movement to *your* day that are not in your daily routine.

   a. _____

   b. _____

I can't count the number of times over the years that my elderly patients said to me, "Don't get old." I would smile at that statement and we would start talking about the medical conditions and feelings that prompted the remark. It seems like a funny statement because we all know that aging is not an option.

However, recently, one of my patients was reflecting on her past life of raising a family, having a loving marriage, thriving in her work, and having fulfilling hobbies. She was not very pleased her health had taken a turn for the worse, and she lost her independence. She leaned over to me and said, "The secret is, don't get old."

There is no magic elixir. The only way we can avoid getting old is to work on staying young. The next four chapters give you the method and directions to put the best therapeutic practices into place to help you and your parents *stay young*. As you are working with your parents during this phase of building exceptional experiences, remember—Don't get old!

16

STEP 1—WHO I AM

*Your vision will become clear only when you can look into
your own heart. Who looks outside dreams;
who looks inside, awakes.*

—Carl Jung

The first step of your adventure with therapeutic encounters is self-awareness. Begin by having a conversation with your parents to explain that you would like to assist them with activities to keep their body, mind, and spirit in optimal shape as they age. Let them know that this is a practice everyone needs to embrace throughout their lifetime through exercises and using healthy lifestyle tools. Explain the process in as much detail as necessary by taking examples from what you have learned in this book. Help them understand that the earlier they start this process, the better chance they have of functioning at their highest physical and mental capacity while living an independent life. This would be an excellent time to provide examples of their peers who are successfully aging.

Determine if they are interested and agree to take part in the therapeutic encounters. Make sure they know they are a part of goal-setting and planning the therapeutic encounters. If you are assisting them remotely, you can explain the process to them and then help them get set up to work on therapeutic encounters with the assistance of others who live close to them. When you both agree it's time to start the four-step method, you can move forward. Plan the first therapeutic encounter together.

If you get a negative response initially from your parent, continue to have conversations and find a way to demonstrate what you are talking about to clear up any confusion. Present them with articles about exercise and nutrition so they can start to educate themselves on the concepts related to healthy living. Professionals who specialize in nutrition, exercise, and other health practices can be consulted to talk to your parents about the benefits of their specialty if needed.

Once your parent agrees to move forward, describe the first step of the process as looking back into their past to reflect on who they are and what strengths they possess. Let them know you respect their likes, dislikes, strengths, weaknesses, dreams, desires, motivations, goals, and unique background. Share a story from your own life, such as a significant accomplishment, to start the conversation. Then ask them to share a story from their past. The first part of this activity focuses on talking about how they grew to become who they are today. Make this a conversation, not a workbook experience. Here are a list of potential questions and topics to get you started as you talk to your parents.

Step 1 conversation:

- What was your favorite cultural heritage tradition in your family as you grew up?

- Who are the people who helped you become who you are today?
- Name a strength you possess.
- What one word best describes you?
- Tell me about a time when you had to overcome an obstacle in your life.
- Share a memory about an experience that made you feel good about yourself.
- What event in your life made a significant impact and brought you joy?

As they tell you stories and answer a few of the questions, listen for the strengths and values they possess. Take note of these attributes. You can then use these words to affirm them during the activities. For instance, let's say your dad was diagnosed with bone cancer when he was nine years old. He went through surgery and treatments, had to take time off of school, and was bedridden for eight months. He fought back to overcome this illness and rebounded to become eligible for the state track meet during his sophomore year of high school. You can point out to him that he possesses courage, persistence, a strong will, an exceptional work ethic, and leadership skills. Remember to refer back to these terms when he is working toward his goals. Giving positive reinforcement by naming his strengths will help him embrace the confidence he needs to continue working toward his goals.

After you have had a chance to reflect on the positive attributes of your parents and name their strengths, you can begin working on a physical activity or exercise. As you plan the activity, make use of your knowledge of the intelligences, sensory experiences, healthy living tools, and exercise options to make the time spent beneficial and fun. Proficiency in this process improves as you practice building the experiences. The worksheet below includes all of the topics covered in the previous chapters. It is not necessary to use all of them during each encounter. Get feedback from your parent on how much activity they can tolerate in one session. You may have to decrease the time spent in the activity to accommodate for their endurance level. After each therapeutic encounter, use some of the outlined questions and comments below as you take time to talk about their experience.

STEP 1 EXCEPTIONAL EXPERIENCE

The planned activity: _____

Intelligences: _____

Sensory stimulation: _____

Physical exercise: _____

Breathing exercise: _____

Meditation: _____

Experiential learning: _____

Brain exercise: _____

Education: nutrition/food_____hydration_____sleep_____

Other: _____

Reflection:
- What did you like about the activity? What didn't you like?
- Tell me what you love about your favorite talent, attribute, or strength.
- Were you able to use that strength during your activity today?
- How can we incorporate your strengths into your activities?

- Did you find a weakness or challenging part of an activity you need to address?

Processing:
- You have strengths, weaknesses, character, hobbies, friends, family, cultural heritage, and experiences that have made you who you are.
- Your strengths, talents, and attributes help you succeed in the present and future.
- You can make choices every day to use your best skills during daily activities.
- You can choose to have a new beginning every day.

Generalizing:
- You have made it to this stage in your life through the good times and challenging seasons.
- Aging is a natural process.
- Exercises for your body and mind assist you to achieve a successful aging experience.

Application:
- Life is a journey that started long ago. You can choose to continue to use your strengths to make the most out of every day of your life.
- Aging brings "mixed blessings" of new experiences into your life. Enjoy your life by participating in activities that help you function to the best of your ability.
- Continuing the process of therapeutic encounters will be beneficial for your mind, body, and spirit.

Congratulations! You have made it through Step 1. Remember that this is a dynamic process. Spend more time in this stage until you and your parents are ready to move on to Step 2 of the process.

17

STEP 2—LIFE VISION AND GOAL SETTING

Vision is the art of seeing what is invisible to others.

—Jonathan Swift

The goal of Step 2 is to help your parents realize or create a vision for the future and set goals to make that vision a reality. Start this therapeutic encounter by having a conversation with your loved ones about their current status regarding mobility, social interactions, activity level, and interests. Talk about the strengths they possess that affect their life as well as the challenges they face. Ask them what they would like to achieve during the rest of their life. If your parents have lost sight of their deepest desires, you may have to help them identify their vision or their purpose in life at this time.

The conversation you have highlights their strong points, and also sheds light on their limitations. As they look toward their future and set goals, this is an opportunity to choose activities that have a positive impact on their body, mind, and spirit. Use some of the following questions as guidelines for your conversation.

Step 2 conversation:

- What is something that you would like to do today if you had no limitations?
- Whom would you like to visit if you had the chance?
- What activity would you like to see yourself accomplish in the next few months?
- Is there something you feel compelled to do during the rest of your life?
- Have you started a project that you would like to complete?
- What is important to you in your life right now?
- Is there an activity that you would like to be able to do better?

After your conversation, let your parents know that you would like to help them set goals for their future. Explain goal setting in simple terms. Use the format outlined in Chapter 14 and a journal or notebook to get started.

If you have a goal in mind for them, ask them if they agree with your idea. Set personal goals for yourself before this session, so you have control over your time and have boundaries set for yourself. Work on setting goals for your parents with their assistance. Make sure to include goals for activities they do on their own or with others.

If you find that your goals are miles apart from your parents, plan to do some compromising, creative thinking, or reach out for professional help. Use the expertise of a physical or occupational therapist to set mobility and cognitive goals. Start writing goals before the activity begins or during the reflection period following the activity.

STEP 2 EXCEPTIONAL EXPERIENCE

The planned activity: _____

Intelligences: _____

Sensory stimulation: _____

Physical exercise: _____

Breathing exercise: _____

Meditation: _____

Experiential learning: _____

Brain exercise: _____

Education: nutrition/food_____hydration_____sleep_____

Other: _____

Reflection:
- Tell me about a time in your life when you had to set a goal.
- What did you achieve as you worked toward that goal?
- Name two goals that you would like to accomplish in the next three months.
- Write two to three long-term goals in a journal.
- Make three short-term goals for every goal you have written as "steps" toward the long-term goal.
- Under each short-term goal, place three activities that you need to work on to achieve the goal.

Processing:
- There are activities you want to do, places you would like to visit, and tasks you want to accomplish for a purpose-filled life.

- To achieve these goals, you need to work on the activities that support them.
- Setting goals is an integral part of your life so that you can reach your full potential and live life to the fullest. Goals give you direction and provide structure for everyday life.

Generalizing:
- Goals change as you progress through different phases of life.
- Goals help you achieve tasks, which are necessary for a successful life.
- There are family members, friends, and others who will work with you to help you achieve the goals you have set.

Application:
- Make a list of activities and adventures directed toward achieving your goals.
- Plan a time to work on the goals through activities during therapeutic encounters.
- Prompt your parents to ask for help during activities as needed to meet short-term and long-term goals.

18

STEP 3—EMPOWERMENT THROUGH CONCRETE ACTIVITIES

Life isn't about finding yourself. It's about creating yourself.

—*George Bernard Shaw*

This step is about looking deeper into the activities that propel your parents to a higher level of function. Let them know they have started on the right path. Discuss how they have discovered their strengths and weaknesses, set goals for the future, and have started the therapeutic experiences. Now it's time to talk in more detail about the specific activities that help them move forward.

Talk to your parents about the benefits of exercise:

- Increase cardiovascular (heart) health
- Keep muscles flexible
- Increase muscle strength

- Improve blood flow to all parts of the body including the brain
- Keep internal organs healthy
- Decrease stress and improve mood and outlook
- Improve balance and decrease the risk of falls

Discuss how they can empower themselves to become active. Ask your parents what they should do to make the changes they desire.

Step 3 conversation:

- What areas of your body do you need to stretch and strengthen?
- Do you need help identifying how you should proceed with exercises?
- How many days a week will you exercise?
- How will you bring socialization into your weekly schedule?
- What exercise can you do for your heart this week?
- What barriers keep you from exercising?
- Do you need to get assistance from a professional such as a physical therapist or professional trainer?

STEP 3 EXCEPTIONAL EXPERIENCE

The planned activity: _____

Intelligences: _____

Sensory stimulation: _____

Physical exercise: _____

Breathing exercise: _____

Meditation: _____

Experiential learning: _____

Brain exercise: _____

Education: nutrition/food___hydration/water_____sleep___

Other: _____

Reflection:
- What was your activity level the past month?
- What did you feel in your muscles as you did the exercises today?
- Did you feel fatigued or short of air?
- What are your main reasons for starting or continuing an exercise program?

Processing:
- Exercise is beneficial in many ways to our mind, body, and spirit.
- Make time to participate in an exercise program to gain health and mobility.
- Identify and make plans to overcome the barriers to starting and staying on an exercise program.

Generalizing:
- Exercise is an essential part of taking care of your health.
- The benefits of exercise include_____
- Now you have an exercise program. Empower yourself to take ownership of it.
- Your exercise program will help you meet your goals of _____

Application:
- Set up or refine an exercise program based on current ability level and needs.
- Help your parents get rid of the barriers to exercising.
- Make sure your parents have the equipment, supportive shoes, weights, and other materials to be successful.
- Make a list with your parents, of ways to empower them to be active.

19

STEP 4—ASSESSING THERAPEUTIC ENCOUNTERS AND GOALS

*Our goals can only be reached through a vehicle of a plan,
in which we must fervently believe, and upon which we
must vigorously act. There is no other route to success.*

—Pablo Picasso

The fourth step of the process involves assessing the therapeutic encounters you have been providing or that you have set up for your parents through outside resources. Evaluate the effectiveness of the experiences. Determine if you see desirable changes in your parents' health and well-being and satisfaction during the activities.

Are the short-term goals met? How much progress did your parents make toward long-term goals? Is it time to re-evaluate the goals and make changes or keep working toward them? Are obstacles getting in the way of completing the therapeutic encounters? If you are finding barriers or roadblocks to your plan that you and your parents cannot overcome, consider talking to a professional to determine if there is a change you need to make.

Step 4 Conversation:

- Assess the goals by looking at your journal and a calendar to determine if you are on track with your program. Talk with your parents about their goals.
- Does the exercise program include stretching, strengthening, cardiovascular or aerobic exercise, brain or mental exercise, relaxation, and breathing exercises?
- Ask your parents if they have the right amount of assistance with their therapeutic encounters and other activities throughout the week.
- Assess your parents' exercise programs and therapeutic activities to find out if they are still appropriate. Do they need to be upgraded or downgraded?
- Write goals to reflect changes in existing goals or to set new goals. Remove goals that are not applicable to your parents' life vision and needs.

STEP 4 EXCEPTIONAL EXPERIENCE

The planned activity: _____

Intelligences: _____

Sensory stimulation: _____

Physical exercise: _____

Breathing exercise: _____

Meditation: _____

Experiential learning: _____

Brain exercise: _____

Education: nutrition/food___hydration/water_____sleep___

Other: _____

Reflection:
- Name an experience that has been particularly helpful to you during this process.
- What activities would you like to continue on your path to successful aging?
- Can you think of someone who needs help with their journey in life?

Processing:
- You have gone through a period working on therapeutic encounters with activities geared toward reaching your highest potential.
- Aging is a process. Assess your physical and mental status and make goals based on your wants and needs for the present and future.
- Every day is an opportunity for you to feel empowered to live life to the fullest.
- As your brain changes with more experience, you need to reassess your feelings, desires, and goals.
- What can you do to thank those who assist you?
- How can you help others reach their goals for healthy living?

Generalizing:
- Aging is a part of life which provides the benefits of wisdom, insight, and strength.
- Illness and a decrease in function can happen to all of us.
- You can choose to empower yourself to combat this decline and accept what you cannot change.
- You can help your situation by having a positive attitude, setting goals, and working toward those goals with determination and joy.

Application:
- Think about how you want to work on your plans for successful aging.
- Recall all of the exercises you have done that benefitted you and think of ways you can incorporate them into your everyday activities.
- Read a bit of your journal and be proud of all of the work you have done so far.
- Reach out to a friend or family member and thank them.
- Give back today with a simple gesture of kindness and feel the warmth of your act.

Summary:
- Congratulate yourself on working through the four-step method!
- Focus on what you've accomplished as you improved the health of your body, mind, and spirit.
- Keep an open mind as you proceed into the future and build additional exceptional experiences.

PART FOUR:

THE LAUNCH

20

ADVANTAGES OF GROUP
THERAPY

Alone we can do so little; together we can do so much.

—Helen Keller

T he end of the book is nearing, and before we go any
further, I want to say that I've been told some heart-
warming stories from friends and family as well as
from individuals I have just met who are building incredible
therapeutic encounters for their loved ones. I am deeply
moved as I see the care, concern, and love that is not only
being passed down through older generations but initiated by
younger generations to positively impact all ages.

Due to my poor technical skills with technology, I am
on the phone frequently with support staff from a variety of
companies. I apologize to all of the employees and IT technicians I have frustrated. You never let on that my ignorance
caused you angst. I'm sure there were plenty of happy hours
that sprung up after solving dilemmas like mine. I hope you
had a good time with your co-workers and were able to put

people like me, who mean well but don't have a clue about technical knowledge, into perspective. You are always more than courteous and helpful. Thank you!

As we work through issues to keep my technology up and running, there is often a lull in the conversation. The technicians, who have excellent training in customer service, strike up a conversation, which usually involves talking about the project I'm working on that needs the technical support. I share that I'm writing a book and they ask what the book entails. As I explain the book to them, they are more than willing to tell me their stories.

One young person told me that his family was helping his grandfather, who lived in another state. They were in the process of planning a visit during the upcoming holiday, and it was his job to pick his grandfather up from the train station. He noted that his balance was not too sharp lately and he hoped that his grandfather would be safe getting from one point to the other. I gave recommendations on safety and assistive devices for walking and stair climbing.

As the conversation progressed, he told me that his friend's mother taught art classes to the elderly out of her home. That news sent me into a frenzy of joy, and I told him about the benefits of art for the brain and body. He sincerely acted interested and told me he would pass on that information. I hope he wasn't thinking, *I need a happy hour!* His empathy and willingness to help his family and the effort of the entire family to change work schedules and plan a fun holiday celebration to include his grandfather were impressive.

I sense an immense amount of love, devotion, and commitment from family members of older adults. There is a family that works together to offer assistance to their sister, the primary caregiver of their parents, so that she can go on extended vacations. Several nursing homes I work in have activities once or twice a day that involve using the body and brain while playing fun games, which promote exercise, laughter, and socialization for residents and their families.

There is an endless supply of ideas for activities on the internet. One activity group stacked empty twelve-pack beverage boxes into a tall, life-size tower and played Jenga. Another example is a nursing home that offers residents and visitors a group exercise class led by a staff member and an exercise video. I noted that the staff member took breaks to educate the group with remarks about how the exercises positively affect their brains and bodies.

In two assisted living facilities, the residents were using weights and stretchy bands for exercise and playing physically challenging games as they participated in a group exercise class. I see an increase in dedication to this process among nursing and activity departments who go above and beyond to find fun and challenging activities to get the whole group involved and active using their bodies, brains, and spirits. This effort is encouraging to me and other health professionals as well as families who want to see health promotion for their patients and aging loved ones.

If you haven't noticed, I have a passion for group therapy and similar shared learning experiences! I find it fascinating to watch the dynamics of the group members and what develops from the interactions in the group setting both at work and in social settings. Although I'm an introvert, I enjoy group activities. Even if you choose to be quiet during the group process, there is so much to gain from listening to others converse and watching others move. Did you know that you can make your neural networks stronger just by watching others move?

As you have already learned, studies show that the predictors of longevity may not be what you expect. Recall the village effect from Chapter 2 of this book. In one study, the number one and two factors predicting a long life were not diet or exercise. Instead, the second most significant predictor of longevity was the number of close relationships a person had.

People who would take them to the doctor, visit and listen to their heartfelt stories, or get together to share a meal. The number one predictor of longevity was social integration.[1] This means that a person was in social contact with others many times a day.

The relationships we build in one-on-one and group settings, that we call our weak ties, are so important to our sense of well-being. Joining new groups and enhancing or maintaining the group identification you already belong to have been found to increase satisfaction in life.[2] Staying socially engaged is essential to our personal fulfillment and health.

As you can see from some of the examples in the book, therapeutic groups are often highly organized and formatted to achieve specific goals that are set up by the therapists based on the evaluation and further assessments of the patient. However, groups can also be casual. There are times when people get together to play cards, go out for lunch, or randomly meet to take a walk. These are all examples of group encounters. So the next time your neighbor asks you to go out to lunch or take a walk, please do not think twice. This has been proven to be very good for your health!

Recently, I witnessed two scenarios that impressed me. One was while my husband and I were hiking in the Colorado Rocky Mountains. We encountered three pairs of hikers during our trek up and down the mountain that displayed the perfect example of an exceptional experience. One set was a middle-aged woman and her teenage daughter who were enjoying spending time together as well as exercising. The other two sets took me by surprise. I was amazed to see the much older hikers—at least seventy to ninety years old—making good time as they traversed the mountain. We greeted each other and stopped to rest as they did, sitting on a boulder, taking time to talk about our experience. From my perspective, I could see the aerobic and strengthening exercise, meditation and relaxation, deep breathing, social support, challenging environment, and fun! The immense satisfaction I felt from seeing this perfect aging experience confirmed my belief that this process is beneficial and does work! Most of us won't be hiking up a mountain with our parents, but we can build exceptional experiences that involve movement, adventure, and fun that complement our lifestyle and interests.

The second scene was at an outdoor amphitheater concert. A terrific blues band was playing. There was plenty of space between the audience and the band for a dance floor and dancing was encouraged. The first dancer to take the floor was a woman who appeared to be in her early 70s. She approached the dance floor standing tall with her elbows flexed, *as cute as a button,* dressed in her neon pink athletic shoes and matching workout clothes. Her movements displayed purpose as she started marching forward then backward. She threw in the grapevine move, twirled around, and started the routine all over. The dancing continued periodically between her rest breaks, and several other dancers in all age ranges eventually joined her. It was turning into a group! I wanted to run down the stairs to tell her all of the marvelous things she was doing for her brain, body, and vestibular system. Instead, I nudged my husband and said, "That's what my book is about!"

As you go through your day, see how many group experiences you can identify while shopping, worshiping, working, and in your family's daily life. You and your parents may be able to have a small cooking group one evening with your family based on a new recipe you would like to try. Now that you know the benefits of group therapeutic encounters, you can use your time together and turn it into a therapeutic experience.

All things in life have positive and negative attributes, and group therapeutic encounters are not exempt.

Some of the benefits of group interactions include the following:

- Experiencing a sense of belonging
- Having opportunities to give and get advice
- Increasing in self-confidence
- Practicing skills in front of peers
- Finding opportunities to communicate

These are a few reasons why your parents many not like group interactions:

- They might have social phobias
- They could experience personality conflicts in a group setting
- They may not want to commit to attending group activities on a regular basis

One day at work, I had the opportunity to get a small group together. I gathered four participants of varying levels of functional abilities. One of the patients was not interested in therapy, but she needed the mobility skills we wanted to teach her to be able to return home. Another woman had suffered a stroke, which took away the left side of her body as far as function. She did not even know the left side of her body existed. The other two were interested in therapy and were steadily progressing their status of mobility.

I pulled over a child-sized basketball hoop and found a plastic ball and a balloon to use to work on endurance, balance, and strength. Again, I was amazed at the power of group therapy. The patient who was not interested in therapy started teaching the woman who had the stroke. She demonstrated batting the balloon to another resident. As she was partaking in the therapeutic activity, she was doing the exercises she needed to do for herself. She also was able to motivate the woman who had the stroke to look to her left side. The woman with the stroke was assisted to use both of her arms in the activity. The other two participants acted as role models when they made basketball shots from seated and standing positions, which improved their balance and muscle strength.

Overall, this group functioned at a high level, bringing everyone to their maximum potential that day with thinking skills, motor skills, and communication. The point of this story is that sometimes the best activities happen with very little planning. By getting a group together to participate in a stimulating activity, they can use their strengths to help themselves and others.

Here are some suggestions of group encounters you could set up in your home with family members during holiday celebrations or family gatherings.

COOKING GROUP

Instead of ordering a take-out pizza, make one with the family. Rolling out the dough, shredding cheese, and cutting up vegetables can be turned into an exercise. It takes more endurance and muscle strength to stand up at the kitchen counter to make a meal. If your parents can't stand for an extended period, sit together as a group around a table to prepare the food. Offer an educational moment such as fun facts about cooking, exciting chefs, meals from around the world, interesting cookbooks, and favorite family meals. Involve your parents in conversation about their history of cooking and related topics.

DECORATING THE DINING ROOM

I find this group experience is one of my favorites because there are so many physical challenges, and it gives people a festive environment for dining and socializing. Holidays such as Valentine's Day and St. Patrick's Day are fun to decorate for and celebrate. The group activity engages individuals by using their motor skills, cognitive skills, and social skills as they work on activities together to transform the dining room into a festive party room.

The supplies I use are an air pump that you manually step on to blow up balloons, streamers, poster boards, ribbons for tying balloons together, scissors, scotch tape, markers, crayons, and window cling sticker decorations.

Set up stations in the dining room for each activity. In one area, your parent can stand up and use the foot pump to blow up the balloons. They may need to have assistance or steady themselves with a walker or table top as it takes balance and strength to stand on one leg while stepping on the pump. Those who cannot stand well can tie balloons together on a long ribbon to be hung up. Another station involves making small posters or Valentine's cards that are placed on the windows or tables. Streamers are cut and draped wherever the room allows.

CARNIVAL DAY

This activity may sound childish, but isn't there a kid in all of us? Who would pass up carnival games and treats? This is a fun and energizing activity to do with a group of people, young and old. In the past, I had access to a variety of games including bean bag toss, Velcro dart game, ring toss, water balloon toss (outdoors), and a small plastic swimming pool to fish out plastic ducks. Set up the games so that there are challenges for balance, coordination, and building strength.

Keep scores for each person on an individual card and when the games end award the highest scoring individual with a prize. Provide treats that you would find at a carnival. There are many ways to make this fun, including carnival music!

CELEBRATE A HOLIDAY—JULY FOURTH PARADE

Patriotic celebrations can be fun. Are there children in the family who have fun decorating their bicycles, tricycles, and wagons before joining in on a festive parade? Make this an activity for your parents as they help the children decorate their bicycles or have them decorate their walker or wheelchair. I have used streamers woven in the spokes of the wheelchair tires, decorative garland wire around the walker frames, small posters hanging from their walkers with patriotic messages, balloons, and flags.

Play patriotic music as you partake in movement activity on your patio, sidewalk, or driveway. Have a snack or barbeque dinner to end the day. Ask your parents to tell stories of how they spent their July 4th or other patriotic celebrations during their childhood and adult years.

Here are some other ideas:

- Bring a joke book to your coffee group—laughter is the best medicine!
- Set up an obstacle course
- Play a game standing at the counter (with good posture)
- Take a nature walk
- Plan a scavenger hunt
- Take a road trip
- Plan an adventure
- Make a bucket list—things you want to accomplish—and go for it!

The examples above will help you start to think of beneficial group experiences your parents and family members would enjoy.

21

CELEBRATE THE CULTURE: THE *WHY* AND THE *WHY NOT*

The greatest healing therapy is friendship and love.

—Hubert H. Humphrey

A few months ago, while I was working with a patient on exercises to stretch his legs, a physician walked into the hospital therapy gym with a group of doctors and residents. They stopped and looked around at the activity going on. He turned to them and said, "This is the culture of therapy."

At that moment, I could *feel* the culture surrounding me. I feel it every time I walk up to a patient, greet them, start to evaluate their present condition, and plan my therapy session. It is present in my colleagues who arrive at work excited to take on the day and make a difference in the lives of their patients. As therapists, we not only go through a rigorous education to be able to be a part of a healing profession, but we also learn to open our hearts and lives daily to our patients. We show up each day to offer a gift.

Think of the gift we offer as a beautiful package, lovingly wrapped in exquisite paper, tied with a shiny ribbon, and completed with a perfect bow on top. It is a present offered to others of hope and restoration because we genuinely care about their well-being. We give them the gift and ask them to untie the ribbon, open up the box, and accept the gift of healing. We want to give them this opportunity to improve their lives by overcoming a physical disability. We, as therapists, have a special calling to help others gain back a part of their life that was taken away by injury, pain, or illness.

I believe in the culture of therapy. I reflected on the statement the doctor made, and I felt proud of the profession and the professionals I work with who go above and beyond in the interest of the patient with the intent of changing one life at a time. The positive attitudes, laughter, understanding, camaraderie, and healing shared within a dedicated group of therapists turn out to be my therapy. When I am in the right environment and get into flow as a therapist, I feel healing in my body.

If there is a glamorous side to the profession, that would be it. There are warm and wonderful feelings you receive from helping others and when a patient has success, it makes your heart sing. I would be sugar-coating the work that is done every day if I did not mention all of the challenges that go into patient care, and that you will experience during caregiving for your parents.

You will find that you become your parents' advocate. You will *go to bat* for them and maybe even *take one for the team*. You will find strengths in yourself that you may never have known to exist.

As a therapist, I believe being an advocate for the patient is the best part of my job. It is very satisfying to know that your patient has what they need to succeed in life to gain optimal health and function.

As we go about doing our job, we run into the good times as well as the bad. We have all had experiences that make us feel numb such as finding out your patient has just received the diagnosis of a terminal illness, and you recall she has four young children at home. Or, sometimes we have to be honest with the patients who need to hear the truth or decrease our expectations when we could tell that we wanted the healing more for our patients than they did—and that can be difficult.

Watching a rodent run through a house and being threatened with a baseball bat weren't exactly the highlights of my career. However, that did not scare me away from being hopeful that the next situation would be better—and it was. It's not easy managing a chest tube, catheter, oxygen tank, IV pole, and abdominal drain while keeping the patient safe during gait training. Yes, there is a certain amount of stress, and not much glamour in the job. Thanks to the co-workers, support staff, and dedicated nursing departments for making my job easier and giving the patients their whole heart and soul in the name of healing.

My hope for you is that you gain a love for the culture of caregiving as you assist your parents to achieve a healthier state. I also want you to experience healing in your body, mind, and spirit as you learn the principles, apply them to your life, and teach them to your parents through therapeutic experiences.

From all of the reading and worksheet exercises you did while reading this book, did you feel a culture of caring for someone that provides concern, assistance, innovation, and fun? You now have an opportunity to start implementing the learning theories, sensory stimulation, healthy living tools, and activities with your parents and loved ones. You are creating your story and journey. Write down some of the funny and exciting things that happen! Quotes from your parents that provide a bit of wisdom, sarcasm, humor, or raw feelings about what they are experiencing will be a treasure for you later in your life.

My father left his five daughters with much wisdom in the small quotes he provided for us. He spared us the long, boring lectures, but did make sure he shared bits of wisdom that had enough impact to lead us down life's path with one of the most important things in life: the truth. When I get together with my sisters, and we reminisce about dad, we are amazed at his insight into the truth. He always valued family and faith above everything else in life. He displayed this in his role as a good, caring father and loving husband even at the end of his life as he battled Alzheimer's disease.

My family chose our *why*. We do what we can to honor our parents out of love, duty, and responsibility. My husband said it very simply in four words, "Go help your mother." We found our why.

What about the *why not*? Why not celebrate every moment in the present? That is one thing my husband, children, and family taught me. Celebrate right now—all the time. View the situation you are in and see the art in it. Appreciate it for what it is and bring it to life. We never had to look for a reason to celebrate life. It existed all around us in our family, which resulted in much singing and dancing in our home. *Why not?*

As my dad lay dying in a bed in the nursing home, he was surrounded by his wife, five daughters, and other family members. We did what we were taught to do—celebrate! We brought in the Irish music my dad loved, trays of food, and blankets to keep us warm as we each took turns to stay by his side. We shared in each other's emotions, sang, danced, laughed, cried, and said our heartfelt goodbyes to dad while celebrating his life. My father couldn't have been a wealthier man than during the moments his family surrounded him with true love. We will never know what he thought of the commotion until we meet again. I hope he was proud and fulfilled during his final hours.

How do you celebrate life? If you aren't in the practice of celebrating, this is an excellent time to start. One way we like to celebrate is to gather together for a family meal. I've had several recommendations to put recipes in this book. If you stretch your imagination, you will find these recipes have some therapeutic value. You won't find them in the Mediterranean diet, but you can use moderation and make them a treat.

My brother-in-law suggested I put my homemade Bloody Mary Mix recipe in because some people may need it after taking care of their parents. Haha! He is one of the many joke-makers in the family. Serve the beverage with or without alcohol. It has a massive boost of Vitamin C and alerts your brain by waking up your sense of taste and smell. Get ready to pucker up!

After reading a couple of chapters of my manuscript, my son dramatically said, "Mom, will you *just* put a cookie recipe in your book, so I know what to do." The cookies that made a big hit with kids and parents during the years my children were involved in athletic games and practices were my monster cookies. Although I cannot take the credit for developing the recipe, I can put it into my famous list as it was regularly requested. I prefer to reduce them to half the size and get them into the freezer as quickly as I can to minimize the temptation. Hope this helps, Alex!

I want to add a recipe you can make with your parents during a therapeutic encounter. How about a traditional meatloaf? The real reason I make meatloaf is to have leftovers for sandwiches. They are the best! So here you go—a few recipes to help you with your celebration of life.

Teresa's Infamous Bloody Mary Mix

Ingredients:

4 c. tomato juice
Juice from 2 freshly squeezed lemons
Juice from 1 freshly squeezed lime

1 tsp. ground pepper (or more)
Kosher or celery salt to taste
½ tsp. cayenne pepper
3 T. Worcestershire sauce
2 T. prepared horseradish
10 dashes of hot pepper sauce (or more)

Mix all ingredients together and refrigerate. Serve with green olives and a celery stick. Use mixture within two to three days. Makes three to four drinks.

Teresa's Famous Monster Cookie Recipe

Ingredients:

½ pound of butter (2 sticks)
1 pound of brown sugar (2 1/3 c.)
2 c. white sugar
6 eggs
1 T. white corn syrup
4 tsp. baking soda
3 c. peanut butter
½ pound M&M'S®
½ pound chocolate chips
1/8 c. vanilla
9 c. oatmeal
(No flour)

In a large mixing bowl, beat together the butter and sugar. Add and beat in the eggs, one at a time. Add and blend the corn syrup, baking soda, vanilla, and peanut butter. Fold in the chocolate chips, M&M'S®, and oatmeal. Drop by large spoonfuls onto a cookie sheet. (I usually make mine ½ the size of a regular monster cookie). Bake at 350°F for 7 to 10 minutes or until lightly browned.

Teresa's Family Favorite Meatloaf Recipe:

Ingredients:

1 ½ pound of lean ground beef
¾ c. ketchup
1 egg
2 T. yellow mustard
1 ½ T. Worcestershire sauce
½ c. onion—grated or very finely chopped
1 T. prepared horseradish
2 T. stone ground mustard
3 T. spicy BBQ sauce
1 tsp. ground pepper
Salt to taste
1 ½ c. fine bread crumbs or cracker crumbs
2 T. water

Mix all of the ingredients in a large bowl, *except* the meat and cracker or bread crumbs, until well combined. Add the meat and bread crumbs and stir until it is well blended. Place the mixture into a casserole dish that is larger than the meatloaf. Shape into a loaf—bake at 350°F for 1 to 1 ¼ hour. The meatloaf should be cooked through to an internal temperature of 160°F.

22

THE SEND OFF—BON VOYAGE

Twenty years from now, you will be more disappointed by the things you didn't do than those you did. So throw off the bowlines. Sail away from safe harbor. Catch the wind in your sails. Explore. Dream. Discover.

—Mark Twain

This is the end of me telling my story and sharing my passion for building exceptional experiences. I hope that after reading this book, you will able to see through your eyes, hear through your ears, feel through your hands, sense through your muscles, and taste and smell the joys and defeats of the human condition. And from this, know we are all traveling on an imperfect journey. As we put one foot ahead of the other, we know we need the presence of people to fill our lives with love and surprise and acceptance and excitement and patience and laughter and experiences.

Now your adventure is beginning. I will step away from the helm of the boat and let you take over. I will also pass the torch to you to carry into the future to light your path as you create exceptional experiences that transform others and yourself.

I want to thank you for participating in this most important adventure of caring for another. It is not always easy, but it is something you can do using wisdom and grace. You are strong enough to embrace this adventure. Remember to pack, staff, and steer your boat wisely. Set boundaries and limits and make sure you are taken care of—and then you can take care of others.

There will be unknown adventures ahead that may seem a bit scary. When turbulent seas beset you—stop, breathe, evaluate your circumstances, and ask for help if you need it. You are heading in the right direction. You are assisting yourself and your loved ones to gain improved health and function. Don't waste time doubting yourself.

I hope as you finish this book and ask yourself what it was all about, you can answer with one word: Love. It was about love.

Now take a bottle of bubbly, break it over the bow of your boat, and sail away on your unique adventure with your loved ones. Look for the ships that pass by on a similar route. They need a friendly smile and wave.

Godspeed, my friend.

The end.

NOTES

CHAPTER 2

[1] Pinker, Susan, *The Village Effect: How Face-To-Face Contact Can Make Us Healthier and Happier.* (Canada, Vintage Canada, 2015), 290.

[2] *Ibid.*, 38-43.

[3] Sandstrom, Gillian M., and Elizabeth W. Dunn. "Social Interactions and Well-Being." *Personality and Social Psychology Bulletin* 40, no. 7 (2014): 910-22. doi:10.1177/0146167214529799.

[4] Bhatti A, (January 24, 2017) The Pathophysiology of Perceived Social Isolation: Effects on Health and Mortality. Cureus 9 (1): e994. D0110.7759/cureus.994.

[5] "The secret to living longer may be your social life." TED/2017, Pinker, Susan, April/2017; https://www.ted.com/talks/susan_pinker_the_secret_to_living_longer_may_be_your_social_life.

[6] "Work and the Loneliness Epidemic." Harvard Business Review. September 05, 2018. https://hbr.org/cover-story/2017/09/work-and-the-loneliness-epidemic.

[7] "New Cigna Study Reveals Loneliness at Epidemic Levels in America." Cigna, a Global Health Insurance and Health Service Company. https://www.cigna.com/newsroom/news-releases/2018/new-cigna-study-reveals-loneliness-at-epidemic-levels-in-america.

[8] Flowers, Lynda, Ari Houser, Claire Noel-Miller, *AARP Public Policy Institute*, Jonathan Shaw, Jay Bhattacharya, Lena Schoemaker, *Stanford University*, and Monica Farid, *Harvard University*. "Medicare Spends More on Socially Isolated Older

Adults." *AARP Public Policy Institute*, November 27, 2017. doi:10.26419/ppi.00016.001.

9   Bredesen DE, Amos EC, Canick J, Ackerley M, Raji C, Fiala M, Ahdidan J. Reversal of cognitive decline in Alzheimer's disease. Aging (Albany NY). 2016; 8:1250-1258.https://doi.org/10.18632/aging.100981.

10 "6 Pillars of Brain Health." Healthy Brains by Cleveland Clinic. https://healthybrains.org/pillars/.

CHAPTER 3

1   *Still Alice*, Directed by Richard Glatzer & Wash Westmoreland, 2014; New York: Sony Pictures, DVD.

CHAPTER 4

1   Family Caregiver Alliance AARP 2015 Report: hppt://www.caregiver.org/caregiver/statistics/demographics.

2   Shapiro, Adam, and Miles Taylor. "Effects of a Community-Based Early Intervention Program on the Subjective Well-Being, Institutionalization, and Mortality of Low-Income Elders." *The Gerontologist* 42, no. 3 (2002): 334-41. doi:10.1093/geront/42.3.334.

CHAPTER 5

1   TED. "Design for All 5 Senses | Jinsop Lee | TED Talks." YouTube. August 06, 2013. https://www.youtube.com/watch?v=N6wjC0sxD2o.

2   Ratey, John J., and Eric Hagerman. *Spark: The Revolutionary New Science of Exercise and the Brain.* New York: Little, Brown, 2013, 222.

3   Kattenstroth JC, Kolankowska I, Kalisch T, Dinse HR. Superior sensory, motor, and cognitive performance in elderly individuals with multi-year dancing activities. *Front Aging Neurosci.* 2010; 2:31. Published 2010 Jul 21. doi:10.3389/fnagi.2010.00031.

4   Ackerman, Courtney. "What Is Neuroplasticity? A Psychologist Explains [14 Brain Plasticity Exercises]." Positive Psychology Program – Your One-Stop PP Resource! February 08, 2019. https://positivepsychologyprogram.com/neuroplasticity/.

[5] Dimeo F, Bauer M, Varaharam I, Proest G, Halter U: Benefits from aerobic exercise in patients with major depression: a pilot study; *Br J Sports Med* 2001;35:114–117.

[6] Park CH, Elavsky S, Koo KM. Factors influencing physical activity in older adults. *J Exerc Rehabil*. 2014;10(1):45–52. Published 2014 Feb 28. doi:10.12965/jer.140089.

CHAPTER 7

[1] "How Packaging Gives Apple's Buyers a Sensory Experience That Reinforces Brand." Personalics. March 15, 2016. https://www.personalics.com/2016/02/03/sensory-design-packaging/.

[2] Hannaford, Carla. *Smart Moves Why Learning Is Not All in Your Head*. Alexander: Great River Books, 2013, 34-37.

[3] *Ibid.*, 34-55.

[4] Schnakers C, Magee WL, Harris B. Sensory Stimulation and Music Therapy Programs for Treating Disorders of Consciousness. *Front Psychol*. 2016; 7:297. Published 2016 Mar 7. doi:10.3389/fpsyg.2016.00297.

[5] "Sensory Stimulation - Alzheimer Society of Manitoba." https://alzheimer.mb.ca/factsheets/Leisureseries/SENSORY STIMULATION.doc.

[6] Harvard Health Publishing. "How Our Senses Change with Age." Harvard Health. https://www.health.harvard.edu/aging/how-our-senses-change-with-age.

[7] Aging Changes in the Senses - Penn State Hershey Medical Center. http://pennstatehershey.adam.com/content.aspx?productId=82&pid=1&gid=004013.

[8] Chanda ML, Levitin DJ. "The neurochemistry of music." Trends Cogn Sci. 2013. Apr;17(4):179-93.

[9] Lin, Frank R., Kristine Yaffe, Jin Xia, Qian-Li Xue, Tamara B. Harris, Elizabeth Purchase-Helzner, Suzanne Satterfield, Hilsa N. Ayonayon, Luigi Ferrucci, Eleanor M. Simonsick, and For the Health Abc Study Group. "Hearing Loss and Cognitive Decline in Older Adults." *JAMA Internal Medicine* 173, no. 4 (2013): 293. doi:10.1001/jamainternmed.2013.1868.

[10] Lin, Frank R. "Hearing Loss and Falls Among Older Adults in the United States." *Archives of Internal Medicine* 172, no. 4 (2012): 369. doi:10.1001/archinternmed.2011.728.

CHAPTER 8

[1]   Gardner, Howard. *Frames of Mind: The Theory of Multiple Intelligences.* New York: Basic Books, 2011.

[2]   *Ibid.*

[3]   Multiple Intelligences—Assessment. https://www.literacynet. org/mi/assessment/findyourstrengths.html.

CHAPTER 9

[1]   Ratey, Spark, 222-223.

[2]   "Exercise, Movement, and The Brain." Psychology Today. https://www.psychologytoday. com/us/blog/ what-body-knows/201511/exercise-movement-and-the-brain.

[3]   Lawrence, Jean. "Train Your Brain with Exercise." WebMD. https://www.webmd.com/fitness-exercise/features/ train-your-brain-with-exercise.

[4]   Griss, Susan. "The Power of Movement in Teaching and Learning." Teacher Teacher. February 19, 2019. https://www. edweek.org/tm/articles/2013/03/19/fp_griss.html.

[5]   Hannaford, *Smart Moves*, 31.

[6]   Oppezzo, Marily, and Daniel L. Schwartz. "Give Your Ideas Some Legs: The Positive Effect of Walking on Creative Thinking." *Journal of Experimental Psychology: Learning, Memory, and Cognition* 40, no. 4 (2014): 1142-152. doi:10.1037/a0036577.

[7]   Mackay, Christopher P., Suzanne S. Kuys, and Sandra G. Brauer. "The Effect of Aerobic Exercise on Brain-Derived Neurotrophic Factor in People with Neurological Disorders: A Systematic Review and Meta-Analysis." *Neural Plasticity* 2017 (2017): 1-9. doi:10.1155/2017/4716197.

[8]   "The Impact of Acute Exercise on Cognitive Function And Brain-Derived Neurotrophic Factor." *The Gerontologist* 56, no. Suppl_3 (2016): 386. doi:10.1093/geront/gnw162.1552.

[9]   Cotman, C. "Exercise: A Behavioral Intervention to Enhance Brain Health and Plasticity." *Trends in Neurosciences* 25, no. 6 (2002): 295-301. doi:10.1016/s0166-2236(02)02143-4.

[10] Erickson, K. I., M. W. Voss, R. S. Prakash, C. Basak, A. Szabo, L. Chaddock, J. S. Kim, S. Heo, H. Alves, S. M. White, T. R. Wojcicki, E. Mailey, V. J. Vieira, S. A. Martin, B. D. Pence, J.

A. Woods, E. Mcauley, and A. F. Kramer. "Exercise Training Increases Size of Hippocampus and Improves Memory." *Proceedings of the National Academy of Sciences*108, no. 7 (2011): 3017-022. doi:10.1073/pnas.1015950108.

[11] Ratey, *Spark*, 40.

[12] Ratey, *Spark*, 5.

[13] Merzenich, Michael, *Brain Plasticity Origins of Human Abilities and Disabilities*, Sixth Symposium, Decade of the Brain Series. NIMH and the Library of Congress. Washington, DC, Feb. 7, 1995.

[14] Calbet, Josep. "The Hebb´s Rule Explained with an Analogy." Neuroquotient. February 08, 2019. https://neuroquotient.com/en/pshychology-and-neuroscience-hebb-principle-rule/.

[15] Merzenich, Michael M. Soft-wired: How the New Science of Brain Plasticity Can Change Your Life. San Francisco: Parnassus, 2013.

[16] *Ibid.*, 158-165.

[17] *Ibid.*, 202-203.

[18] Mahncke, H. W., B. B. Connor, J. Appelman, O. N. Ahsanuddin, J. L. Hardy, R. A. Wood, N. M. Joyce, T. Boniske, S. M. Atkins, and M. M. Merzenich. "Memory Enhancement in Healthy Older Adults Using a Brain Plasticity-based Training Program: A Randomized, Controlled Study." *Proceedings of the National Academy of Sciences*103, no. 33 (2006): 12523-2528. doi:10.1073/pnas.0605194103.

[19] Schmiedek. "Hundred Days of Cognitive Training Enhance Broad Cognitive Abilities in Adulthood: Findings from the COGITO Study." *Frontiers in Aging Neuroscience*, 2010. doi:10.3389/fnagi.2010.00027.

[20] "Flexibility – Go4Life." National Institute on Aging. https://go4life.nia.nih.gov/exercise-type/flexibility/.

[21] "Strength – Go4Life." National Institute on Aging. https://go4life.nia.nih.gov/exercise-type/strength/.

[22] Waehner, Paige. "Cardio Guidelines for Seniors to Start Exercising and Be Healthy." Verywell Fit. June 26, 2018. https://www.verywellfit.com/cardio-exercise-guidelines-for-seniors-1230952.

CHAPTER 10

[1] Kolb, David A. *Experiential Learning: Experience as the Source of Learning and Development.* Englewood Cliffs, NJ: Prentice-Hall, 1984, 38.

[2] Pahomov, Larissa. *Authentic Learning in the Digital Age: Engaging Students through Inquiry.* Alexandria, VA:ASCD, 2014.

[3] Kolb, *Experiential Learning*, 96.

[4] Altermann, Caroline D. C., Alexandre S. Martins, Felipe P. Carpes, and Pamela B. Mello-Carpes. "Influence of Mental Practice and Movement Observation on Motor Memory, Cognitive Function and Motor Performance in the Elderly." *Brazilian Journal of Physical Therapy* 18, no. 2 (2014): 201-09. doi:10.1590/s1413-35552012005000150.

CHAPTER 11

[1] "Capillaries Scramble to Feed Oxygen to Brain." Futurity. August 10, 2016. https://www.futurity.org/brain-oxygen-energy-1221902-2/.

[2] "Breathing Exercises: Three to Try | 4-7-8 Breath | Andrew Weil, M.D." DrWeil.com. January 07, 2019. https://www.drweil.com/health-wellness/body-mind-spirit/stress-anxiety/breathing-three-exercises/.

[3] Serra-Majem, Lluis, and Antonia Trichopoulou. "Updating the Benefits of the Mediterranean Diet: From the Heart to the Earth." *Mediterranean Diet*, 2016, 3-14. doi:10.1007/978-3-319-27969-5_1.

[4] Steffen, Lyn M., David R. Jacobs, June Stevens, Eyal Shahar, Teresa Carithers, and Aaron R. Folsom. "Associations of Whole-grain, Refined-grain, and Fruit and Vegetable Consumption with Risks of All-cause Mortality and Incident Coronary Artery Disease and Ischemic Stroke: The Atherosclerosis Risk in Communities (ARIC) Study." *The American Journal of Clinical Nutrition* 78, no. 3 (2003): 383-90. doi:10.1093/ajcn/78.3.383.

[5] Melinda Smith, M.A., Lawrence Robinson, and Robert Segal, M.A. Last updated: December 2018. The Mediterranean Diet, What You Need to Know About Eating the Mediterranean Way, https://www.helpguide.org/articles/diets/the-Mediterranean-diet-htm?pdf=13138.

NOTES

6   "Alzheimer's: Can a Mediterranean Diet Lower My Risk?" Mayo
    Clinic. February 02, 2018. Accessed April 02, 2019. https://
    www.mayoclinic.org/diseases-conditions/alzheimers-disease/
    expert-answers/alzheimers-disease/faq-20058062.
7   MacGill, Markus. "How Much Water Should I Drink Each
    Day?" Medical News Today. July 09, 2018. Accessed April 03,
    2019. https://www.medicalnewstoday.com/articles/306638.php.
8   Thorpe, Matthew, MD, PhD. "12 Science-Based Benefits of
    Meditation." Healthline. July 05, 2017. https://www.healthline.
    com/nutrition/12-benefits-of-meditation.
9   *Ibid.*
10 Marciniak, Rafał, Katerina Sheardova, Pavla Čermakova,
    Daniel Hudeček, Rastislav Šumec, and Jakub Hort. "Effect
    of Meditation on Cognitive Functions in Context of Aging
    and Neurodegenerative Diseases." *Frontiers in Behavioral
    Neuroscience* 8 (2014). doi:10.3389/fnbeh.2014.00017.
11 *Ibid.*
12 Rosenkranz, Melissa A., Richard J. Davidson, Donal G.
    Maccoon, John F. Sheridan, Ned H. Kalin, and Antoine Lutz.
    "A Comparison of Mindfulness-based Stress Reduction and an
    Active Control in Modulation of Neurogenic Inflammation."
    Brain, Behavior, and Immunity 27 (2013): 174-84.
    doi:10.1016/j. bbi.2012.10.013.
13 Wong, Wee Ping, Jan Coles, Richard Chambers, David Bin-Chia
    Wu, and Craig Hassed. "The Effects of Mindfulness on Older
    Adults with Mild Cognitive Impairment." *Journal of Alzheimers
    Disease Reports* 1, no.1 (2017): 181-93. doi:10.3233/adr-170031.
14 Barnes, Josephine, Jonathan W. Bartlett, Laura A. Van De
    Pol, Clement T. Loy, Rachael I. Scahill, Chris Frost, Paul
    Thompson, and Nick C. Fox. "A Meta-analysis of Hippocampal
    Atrophy Rates in Alzheimers Disease." *Neurobiology
    of Aging* 30, no. 11 (2009): 1711-723. doi:10.1016/j.
    neurobiolaging.2008.01.010.
15 Holzel, Britta K., James Carmody, Mark Vangel, Christina
    Congleton, Sita M. Yerramsetti, Tim Gard, and Sara W. Lazar.
    "Mindfulness Practice Leads to Increases in Regional Brain
    Gray Matter Density." *Psychiatry Research: Neuroimaging*191,
    no. 1 (2011):36-43. doi:10.1016/j.pscychresns.2010.08.006.
16 Schulte, Brigid. "Harvard Neuroscientist: Meditation
    Not Only Reduces Stress, Here's How It Changes Your

209

Brain." The Washington Post. May 26, 2015. https://www.
washingtonpost. com/news/inspired-life/wp/2015/05/26/
harvard-neuroscientist-meditation-not-only-reduce
s-stress-it-literally-changes-your-brain/.

[17] Wong, Wee Ping, Jan Coles, Richard Chambers, David
Bin-Chia Wu, and Craig Hassed. "The Effects of Mindfulness
on Older Adults with Mild Cognitive Impairment." *Journal of
Alzheimers Disease Reports*1, no. 1 (2017): 181-93. doi:10.3233/
adr-170031.

[18] "A Guided Meditation for Resting in the Flow." Mindful. May
29, 2019. https://www.mindful.org/mindful-life-flux/.

[19] Stojanovich, Ljudmila, and Dragomir Marisavljevich. "Stress as
a Trigger of Autoimmune Disease." *Autoimmunity Reviews*7, no.
3 (2008): 209-13. doi:10.1016/j.autrev.2007.11.007.

[20] McLeod, S. A. (2010). Stress, illness and the immune
system. Retrieved from https://www.simplypsychology.org/
stress-immune.html.

[21] Wenger, Elisabeth, Sabine Schaefer, Hannes Noack, Simone
Kuhn, Johan Martensson, Hans-Jochen Heinze, Emrah Duzel,
Lars Backman, Ulman Lindenberger, and Martin Lovden.
"Cortical Thickness Changes following Spatial Navigation
Training in Adulthood and Aging." *NeuroImage* 59, no. 4
(2012): 3389-397. doi:10.1016/j. neuroimage.2011.11.015.

[22] Talks, TEDx. "Forget What You Know | Jacob Barnett |
TEDxTeen." YouTube. April 09, 2012. https://www.youtube.
com/watch?v=Uq-FOOQ1TpE.

[23] *Ibid.*

[24] "Guided Meditations." Guided Meditations – UCLA Mindful
Awareness Research Center - Los Angeles, CA. https://www.
uclahealth.org/marc/mindful-meditations.

[25] "Links to Free Online Guided Meditations." Head in the
Clouds. https://headintheclouds.typepad.com/head_in_the_
clouds/links-to-free-online-guided-meditations.html.

[26] "The Benefits of Slumber." National Institutes of Health.
April 04, 2018. https://newsinhealth.nih.gov/2013/04/
benefits-slumber.

[27] Xie, L., H. Kang, Q. Xu, M. J. Chen, Y. Liao, M. Thiyagarajan,
J. Odonnell, D. J. Christensen, C. Nicholson, J. J. Iliff,
T. Takano, R. Deane, and M. Nedergaard. "Sleep Drives

Metabolite Clearance from the Adult Brain." *Science*342, no. 6156 (2013): 373-77. doi:10.1126/science.1241224.

28 Wenderoth, Nicole. "Motor Learning Triggers Neuroplastic Processes While Awake and During Sleep." *Exercise and Sport Sciences Reviews* 46, no. 3 (2018): 152-59. doi:10.1249/jes.0000000000000154.

29 Dailyhap. "Why Your Brain Needs More Downtime: Scientific American." DailyHap. October 16, 2013. https://dailyhap.tumblr.com/post/64214713608/why-your-brain-needs-more-downtime-scientific.

30 Dailyhap. "Why Your Brain Needs More Downtime: Scientific American."

CHAPTER 13

1 Schumacher, K. L., Jones, P. S., & Meleis, A. I. (1999). *Helping elderly persons in transition: A framework for research and practice*. In Swanson, Elizabeth A., and Toni Tripp-Reimer. *Life Transitions in the Older Adult: Issues for Nurses and Other Health Professionals*. (pp.1-26). New York, NY: Springer Pub., 1999.

2 Bridges, William. *Transitions: Making Sense of Life's Changes*. Cambridge, MA: Da Capo Press, 2009.

3 *Ibid.*, 114.

4 Langner, Suzanne R. "Finding Meaning in Caring for Elderly Relatives: Loss and Personal Growth." *Holistic Nursing Practice*9, no. 3 (1995): 75-84. doi:10.1097/00004650-199504000-00011.

5 Schumacher, K. L., Jones, P. S., & Meleis, A. I. (1999). *Helping elderly persons in transition: A framework for research and practice*. In Swanson, Elizabeth A., and Toni Tripp-Reimer. *Life Transitions in the Older Adult: Issues for Nurses and Other Health Professionals*. (pp. 8-9). New York, NY: Springer Pub., 1999.

6 Bagan, Barbara, PhD, ATR-BC. "Aging: What's Art Got to Do with It?" http://www.todaysgeriatricmedicine.com/news/ex_082809_03.shtml.

7 Cohen, G., (2006). *The creativity and aging study: The impact of professionally conducted cultural programs on older adults, final report*. Washington, DC: National Endowment for the Arts. Retrieved from http://arts.gov/sites/default/files/CnA-Rep4-30-06.pdf.

8   Bagan, "Aging: What's Art Got to Do with It?"
9   Mcfadden, Susan H., and Anne D. Basting. "Healthy Aging Persons and Their Brains: Promoting Resilience Through Creative Engagement." *Clinics in Geriatric Medicine* 26, no. 1 (2010): 149-61. doi:10.1016/j. cger.2009.11.004.
10 Bull, Margaret J. "Managing the Transition from Hospital to Home." Qualitative Health Research 2, no. 1 (February 1992): 27–41. doi:10.1177/104973239200200103.
11 Daly, M. P. and Fredman, L. (1993), Caregiver Stress. Journal of the American Geriatrics Society, 41: 466-467. doi:10.1111/j.1532-5415.1993.tb06967.x.
12 Schumacher, K. L., Jones, P. S., & Meleis, A. I. (1999). *Helping elderly persons in transition: A framework for research and practice.* In Swanson, Elizabeth A., and Toni Tripp-Reimer. *Life Transitions in the Older Adult: Issues for Nurses and Other Health Professionals.* (pp. 8-9). New York, NY: Springer Pub., 1999.
13 "Why We Find Change So Difficult, According to Neuroscience." NBCNews.com. https://www.nbcnews. com/better/health/how-train-your-brain-accept-chang e-according-neuroscience-ncna934011.

CHAPTER 14

1   Doran, G. T. (1981). There's a S.M.A.R.T. Way to Write Management's Goals and Objectives. Management Review, 70, 35-36. - References - Scientific Research Publishing. https:// www.scirp.org/(S(351jmbntvnsjt1aadkposzje))/reference/ ReferencesPapers.aspx?ReferenceID=1459599.

CHAPTER 20

1   Sukhoterina, Yelena. "Yelena Sukhoterina." AltHealthWorkscom RSS2. https://althealthworks. com/15091/ the-top-2-predictors-ofa-long-and-healthy-life-have-noth ing-to-do-withfood-or-exercise-massive-study-revealsyelena/.
2   Knight, Craig, S. Alexander Haslam, and Catherine Haslam. "In Home or at Home? How Collective Decision Making in a New Care Facility Enhances Social Interaction and Wellbeing amongst Older Adults." *Ageing and Society* 30, no. 8 (2010): 1393-418. doi:10.1017/s0144686x10000656.